To: Trina

Best Wishes

Tricia Ferro

LOOK
BOTH ⬍↑ WAYS

9 EVOLUTIONARY PARENTING PRINCIPLES

2013

LOOK BOTH WAYS

9 EVOLUTIONARY PARENTING PRINCIPLES

PARENT WITH POSSIBILITY
IN UNCERTAIN TIMES

TRICIA FERRARA

ARCHWAY
PUBLISHING

Archway Publishing books may be ordered through booksellers or by contacting:

Archway Publishing
1663 Liberty Drive
Bloomington, IN 47403
www.archwaypublishing.com
1-(888)-242-5904

ISBN: 978-1-4808-0203-2 (e)
ISBN: 978-1-4808-0202-5 (sc)
ISBN: 978-1-4808-0201-8 (hc)

Library of Congress Control Number: 2013915727

Printed in the United States of America

Archway Publishing rev. date: 9/12/2013

To all defenseless children who have been
victimized or targeted by violence: may your
experiences and suffering not have been in vain

TABLE OF CONTENTS

FOREWORD

At some point in time, anyone who has a child has pondered, *Shouldn't this little bundle come with instructions?*

Finally Tricia Ferrara has cut through the clutter and raised the bar for parents, providing a clear call to action for parenting to evolve. With a unique perspective that is long overdue, she challenges us to let go of old parenting scripts and unproductive habits and bring forth those that are relevant and necessary to raise kids in today's fast-paced world.

Tricia is passionate about helping us become better parents as she guides us to develop stronger, more meaningful, and lasting connections with our children.

Her nine timeless principles are priceless. I see their value in shaping children's lives every day. They help us cultivate the attitudes in our children that will help them reach their full potentials—empathy, resiliency, accountability, and good judgment.

I have the utmost respect and admiration for Tricia, who runs a flourishing counseling practice and lectures regularly while raising two wonderful children. And I'm thankful that she has boiled down her wealth of knowledge, research, and clinical experience into a book that will serve families well.

As Tricia inspires us to be better parents, I have no doubt her candid approach may shake things up a bit with a dose of reality. But isn't that exactly what we need and want for our families?

Ellen Langas
Author of the *Girls Know How®* series
Youth Career Education Advocate
Haverford, PA

PREFACE

The parent-child relationship is the first chapter of
everyone's story; it is the foundation for the world
we know and the world we will come to know.

My work and life as a therapist over the past decade have positioned me as a hybrid of sorts. I feel part scientist at certain times, part artist at others. As a scientist, I am continually testing theories and hypotheses about what motivates people in life and, conversely, what holds them back. As an artist, I am compelled to hold a vision for others when they have lost the ability to hold their own. My job is to ensure they acquire insight and tools to bring forth a new reality based on that vision.

Every day I am allowed privileged access to witness and participate in the sacred stories of many individuals and families. As I take in and digest their journeys, I am certain with each spoken word that we as a species—not just as a society—are being challenged to evolve and grow to meet the new, complex demands of the twenty-first century.

But it is not solely the life scripts of my clients that concern me—it's the headlines and images beamed by satellite that are increasingly punctuated by loss of security, constant threats, faltering institutions, and unimaginable greed and waste. As I listen, analyze, and observe, it seems the same questions haunt almost every story: Where are we going from here as a culture? As families? As individuals? And could we really screw this up?

Events that previously were rare cultural footnotes have become driving forces for our collective future: violence among and against children, abuse, sexually transmitted disease among teenagers, climate change, crushing financial pressures ... just to name a few.

And so new questions emerge: Where do we go from here? What and who will lead us out of this moment?

Look Both Ways has been rolling around in my head for several years. I'm not exactly sure when the ideas began to take shape. Maybe it was around the obvious inflection points: the stunning explosion of social media, 9/11, Columbine, the Sandy Hook massacre, the shock of underage student/teacher sex scandals, and the spectacular collapse of investment banking all are possible influences. *We're not in Kansas anymore*, I found myself thinking. Something was, and still is, happening all around me. I was sensing a story struggling to be told.

What I sought was the language to describe the moment we were and are still facing, to provide a framework of what has been unfolding so I could address how parents could design, create, and direct a successful future for their children and families.

Slowly but surely, key words began to emerge—adaptability, entrepreneurialism, moral imagination, sustainability, digital, resilience, saliency, viral, exploit, risk, strategy, self-organizing, neural connections, consciousness, and immunity—all parts of a new script, one free of the old fear-based paradigms for child-raising, yet full of *human* connection, creativity, and imagination, which comprise the essential fuel to assimilate this way of thinking.

Look Both Ways weaves these words into a fresh understanding of what we will need to know and are obligated to teach our children. It identifies where we stand on the map of modern society and helps parents connect the dots of new, *relevant* information. Most importantly, it illustrates the most potent message conceivable for our modern day family: childhood is the opening chapter for all our stories. The parent-child relationship is the beginning of everything in this world: the world we know and the world we will come to know and the good, the bad, and the ugly that informs who we are but need not limit who we can be.

There is an ancient Chinese saying to describe the activity of the world: "This arises ... that becomes." It begs the modern day questions: How are we raising our children? What will they become?

Let's take a look and see.

Chester Springs, PA

ACKNOWLEDGMENTS

Every original body of work needs a witness, someone to wait while the artist wrestles with internal resistance and insecurities. Most importantly, it needs someone willing to hold the vision when the writer has lost her own. I owe a deep gratitude to Ellen Langas for believing in my work and providing support and guidance the entire way.

My sister, Maureen Neville, has been holding the door open for this book since the first whisper of its inception. Her unfailing confidence in me, loyalty, and encouragement have made all the difference along the way.

There are also the voices that I have heard but could not see, to whom I owe a great debt. Mary Pipher, author of *Reviving Ophelia*, is one of them. By sounding the call to therapists, she implored us to "change the world at least by our little millimeter every day. If you have any interest at all in writing, I encourage you to give it a try. You have your own voice to offer the world. Show up. Tell your truths. Speak out." It was the energy contained in this statement that fueled the book and helped bring it across the finish line. *Look Both Ways* is the answer to that call.

I. CULTURE

INTRODUCTION: CULTURE

Any belief system must be supported by culture, or it will die.

RIGHT NOW WE ARE IN a cultural twilight. Time-honored ways of living are on the decline while we are tantalized by the possibilities of how our individual and collective futures will unfold.

As parents, we are here to make calculations to help our children stay on course toward their futures. Culture provides that framework. The "cultural scripts" adults write must be pragmatic and real: pragmatic in that they continually crystallize and acknowledge present conditions, and real because they deliver full disclosure of the outcome. The culture we provide for our children must support the belief system that we want them to use as a guide. Any belief system that is not supported by culture will die.

Relying on past assumptions leaves us all unprepared for future challenges. Balancing between past and future is key in any evolving culture. Ideas that have been regarded as good and reasonable for years or even decades may no longer be sufficient or even relevant. At one time, a high school diploma was a ticket to a successful future. Now, achieving nothing beyond that is a stigma and potential life sentence to poverty. Alvin Toffler, author of *Future Shock*, has theorized that "the illiterate of the 21st century will not be those who cannot read or write, but those who cannot learn, unlearn and relearn." Remember the food pyramid that we all grew up with? What we thought we knew about nutrition must be unlearned. For instance, did you know that "fatty food" is the new black? Or that what was once considered "junk DNA" a mere five or so years ago actually plays a major role in our genetic makeup? New ideas and better information are constantly being generated. It is our job to sort through them to bring forward what will work and be sustainable, and leave the rest behind.

The winning culture of the future will focus on its most versatile, valuable asset—*its youth.* To a large extent, our children's success depends on our culture and a new brand of directives that will guide and prepare our children for the future, one that is sure to bring about unwanted influences and unpredictable outcomes and events.

In the coming decades, our cultural script needs to account for a new kind of resilience and skill for managing all types of far-flung information and influences. This reality is compounded when we try to address contemporary challenges with only perspectives from the past. Our kids are particularly vulnerable. The twenty-first century requires parents to be proactive, seeing things from a vantage point where an emerging tomorrow can be anticipated.

We have all felt the cultural jolts that shake us to the core. They are the events that highlight the Achilles' heel of our current beliefs. The attacks on the World Trade Center, Hurricane Katrina, the mortgage and debt crisis, and the sinking of the *Titanic* were all born of failure of imagination, outdated information, and false bravado that resulted in unthinkable outcomes. A huge gap existed between what officials thought could happen and what happened. Confident in their level of precautions, those in control let business as usual rule the day. Sadly, this mindset ultimately paved the way for the unimaginable to unfold right before our eyes.

The "unsinkable" *Titanic* became sinkable when the reckless decision to skimp on building materials collided with unskilled, unprepared responses to the unforeseen—an iceberg whose massive destructive power was not visible to the naked eye.

We entered into all of these situations with unacceptable levels of vulnerability *that were avoidable.*

As parents, we cannot possibly remove all icebergs from the paths of our children; however, we can ask ourselves to acknowledge the important role of our culture as a means to prepare them. Are we ignoring warnings and becoming spectators? Is our culture providing the right building materials so that children and young adults can respond skillfully to the unpredictable, at least until help arrives?

Providing answers to these questions requires that we move to a shared focus of not only prevention, but prediction. Like the weather, the more accurate our forecast, the better prepared families will be to respond.

CULTURE IS AS CULTURE DOES

Our collective behavior determines our culture. Consider how these headlines define today's culture:

- "Teen kills girlfriend, then himself after argument"
- "Investor steals billions in Ponzi scheme; robs generations"
- "Obesity reaches epidemic proportions among children"
- "College grads drowning in credit card debt"
- "Test scores show kids getting dumber"
- "Politician pleads guilty"

Each headline carries the subtext that *we have lost our limits.* Exploiting rich, poor, young, old, unborn, and unarmed has blurred the lines between culture and chaos. In our society, there has been an erosion of our ability to influence our future. One small step that leads to a giant leap for humankind does not happen by accident.

Our choices and defaults today have enormous impact on the tomorrow we craft for our children. The events underlying these headlines were not part of an "immaculate conception" of problems. We participated in their creation. Even as spectators, we play a role in how our culture either helps or hinders. As the grown-ups, how we respond and what we allow inform our children not only of how to live, but of what to permit.

How we educate and what we eat demonstrate some of the most potent examples of how the practices of our culture can enhance tomorrow or cause it to wander off track. Our exuberance to produce efficient processed food turned out to be not only wrong, but deadly. We call obesity an epidemic as though it were the flu and cannot be detected, influenced, or prevented. There was a time when we knew that eight ounces of a soft drink was enough. Now we live with the pretense that a Big Gulp does not carry big consequences. Who would have thought we would have to start a "Just Say No" campaign for food?

We rant about not leaving children behind, when really they stay right here with us regardless of whether or not we properly address their educational needs. There is no way to escape the drag of a poorly educated society.

Rising levels of depression, materialism, and stress among our school-age populations are the wake-up calls that say we must not only revisit where we have been but take charge of where we are going. It won't matter how high SAT scores are or which athletic achievements adorn your children's bedroom walls. Their futures will be made or broken by the tools and worldview we provide for them in the everyday. Can our children sustain relationships and resources with the building materials and tools we are providing? Are we helping them build and grow their characters and personal constitutions? Do they have an accurate worldview to guide them when Mom or Dad is out of reach? This is a tall order, even in my family. The real risk is leaving our children in the dark, unable to respond or adapt to life's ups and downs in a constructive way. Parents certainly cannot expect to have all the answers. But we do have the capacity to design, create, and model behaviors that can put our kids back in the driver's seat and ultimately help them get where they need and want to go.

CHAPTER 1

Family Culture Counts

"Parent" is a verb, not a noun.

ONCE UPON A TIME, WE were taught to believe the "begats" model of evolution. It's an overly simplistic view that projects a straight line toward a more advanced point, touting that as millennia passed, apes became upright to evolve into modern human beings. During the journey, human beings transitioned from prey to predators and took control of their environment. We were thought to have hit the "survival of the fittest" jackpot by being aggressive hunters able to dominate enemies.

Fossils, acting as postcards from the past, paint a completely different picture. As it turns out, the story is far more complex. We not only have a prehistoric family tree, but it's also more like a family forest of distant human cousins that possess varying degrees of physical strength and other modern human traits: upright posture, larger brains, toolmaking capacity. Yet for some reason, their evolutionary paths diverged. Where Homo sapiens moved forward, our "extended family" met dead ends. Murder and mating were thought to be the main forces behind the disappearance of our competition, the Neanderthals; however, anthropological research indicates that a little help from Mother Nature pushed them off the evolutionary fast track. We now know that the earth served up some very cruel extremes of climate changes in her past. Habitats were destroyed, and new ones appeared. Inability to adapt quickly enough to their shifting surroundings was a huge factor in the final knockout punch for our distant cousins, setting the stage for modern humans to thrive and become the dominant players in the animal kingdom.

If we weren't the biggest and strongest, how did we prevail? Apparently, we redrew the map by changing the definition of "fittest." Instead of surviving based on brute force, we spread out and cooperated. The deciding factor was *connection*, not dominance. How we thought about and treated one another in small groups prepared us to weather the perfect storm of environmental changes. A golden age of survival was born through challenge and adversity.

Our ancestors responded to disruptions with focus and flexibility, creating resilience among the small groups. For instance, when the climate changed dramatically, relying on hunting became too risky. In response, foraging was added to the prehistoric menu. Eventually, instead of waiting for the plant life to come to them, modern humans brought the plants to life by developing agriculture and farming through use of tools.

These resilient small groups were the precursors to our modern families. Our DNA still holds their ability to cultivate relationships built on social skill, bonding, trust, diverse talent, and—most importantly—*shared power.*

Just as those small groups were led by the adults on duty, *modern-day parents remain the most powerful agents of change and growth in our families.*

Families today are being threatened by equally fierce evolutionary forces. Mothers and fathers face competition from our informational and technological revolution for the hearts and minds of their children. Families that recognize the importance of creating a culture based on accountability and connection will enter a golden age of the family.

Shifting the gravitational pull from external goals to internal ones will result in a bolstered psychological immunity for everyone. Children and adults will have the opportunity to develop a positive process to cope with change and set the stage for a legacy of resilient relationships founded on possibility and creativity.

FALL OF THE CHILDHOOD EMPIRE

Strong families have always formed a cornerstone of American culture. Many of us were raised by parents who were in command and control. Parents were number one. As adults, what they said or did had merit and value. What children, especially small ones, said or did had little merit or value by comparison. More often than not, family life required children to *live in fear, be invisible, and—in some cases—ignore emotion*. Growing up, most of us feared adults, especially our parents. The personal needs of children were rarely if ever defined, let alone recognized or met. *Emotion* was not only a foreign word, but it was a bad word too, particularly for little boys.

We now know that early imprinting on children has a profound effect on how they navigate relationships later in life. If childhood is filled with interactions that lack connection and expression, then adulthood will look much the same. The dance between domination of and overdependence on loved ones can easily block growth and destroy future relationships. Adults who are unaware of these programmed patterns may march on chronologically, but their relationships will be dominated by the experiences of childhood.

There are countless adults raising children with the notions acquired in their own childhoods. With this in mind, it is amusing to think that not long ago, people were running around looking for their "inner child." My clinical experience confirms that it is the inner *adult* that needs excavating, shedding subconscious beliefs and behaviors acquired in childhood that were limited by fear, invisibility, or stifled emotions.

As parents, we are being charged to grow beyond those limitations so we can foster new competencies in our children.

Sadly, children have become skeptics as we stumble through this process. Many of them no longer believe in the power of the family. A lot has been written about how to respond to every situation, from unruly preschoolers to weapon-toting, sexually promiscuous, back-talking teens. I speak to parents every day who mistakenly believe that these behaviors are just happening now, when in fact, many of them have been generations in the making.

Back in the day, families were not utilized to create healthy relationships. As a matter of fact, most parents behaved as if they had no future with their children. But now, longevity and lifestyle have left them puzzled and perplexed about the strange outcomes for their offspring. Depression, addiction, and divorce, among other challenges, scatter the landscape at an alarming rate. Previous generations had no idea of the essential nature of emotional well-being; rather, they believed good parents merely provided the "coin" currency for the family to literally pay for the shoemaker, grocer, and baker. No one was concerned with the importance of "emotional" currency. Emotional currency is the de facto energy source for personal growth, the polar opposite of the stifling shame and fear that were served up in the past. This notion shatters the image of parents as static entities to be feared or avoided and recasts them as resources who understand that providing emotional currency leads to empathy, innovation, creativity, and resilience.

The adults who conquer the old empire will be prepared to parent a generation whose very survival will depend not only upon the ability to relate to how others feel, but also to develop skills for self-direction. Getting to that point will require accountability on the part of both parents and children.

CHAPTER 2

Parenting: The Next "Killer App"

IT IS THE HOLY GRAIL sought after by half the globe, the next big "killer app," the application download that will change everything and provide the tools to conquer new frontiers. The search need go no further than the backyards, classrooms, and ball fields of the American landscape. Parenting is the next killer application that will flood the marketplace with collaborative, resilient, flexible engineers, artists, leaders, legal minds, and lovers born of a rebooted and refreshed approach to parenting in the twenty-first century.

In a sense, this will be a simple *shift of supply and demand* within our families that leads to dramatic results. To reboot parenting will require a review of the past to determine what stays and what goes in family cultures.

I realize that this challenge comes at a time when the media relentlessly blasts headlines that make parents feel obsolete. Is this media blast due to parent absenteeism? Surprisingly, not at all. In fact, these stories are all occurring at a confirmed peak of parental involvement. I've seen parents hovering to protect their children with everything from contracts for abstinence to bulletproof backpacks.

And more than a few parents have asked, "Why do our children seem so out of reach, so out of control? Are they really that different this time around?"

No, they are not.

The difference is that we can no longer live with the script enjoyed by the Greatest Generation. Taking candy from strangers is the very least of our worries! If an outrageous story about a child as victim or violator surfaced, other adults back then could confidently respond, "Not in our backyards." Moms and dads knew their neighborhoods, where they began and where they ended. They also enjoyed a seat at the top of the hill, an unchallenged position of respect. They felt in control and in the lead.

So what gives?

What has changed is that kids are being fed far too much junk information. That has the power to flatten systems, like families, that once had a built-in hierarchy. Parents of previous generations enjoyed a virtual lock on information; in fact, being its keeper was the foundational pillar of their authority and their ability to dictate what took place in the home. Children knew but a few important snippets that would affect their day-to-day lives—their birthdates, their addresses, how to play tag, and what they would be for Halloween—leaving more than enough room on their radar screens for parents to provide them with directives as needed.

And, for better or worse, that imbalance created a chain of command. Often run by the "DOD" (Department of Dad), traditional nuclear families had the benefit of the myth of an "all-knowing" parent. The advent of cable television, target marketing to kids, the Internet, and myriad technologies have busted that one for good. In a world flattened by a steady stream of audio and video information carrying messages that spread like viruses, what was once the final word from a parent is now just a data point.

By not adapting to the new terrain of parent/child challenges, we participate in their perpetuation. Even as spectators, we play a role of helping or hindering.

That's the bad news. Here's the good: make no mistake about it, in today's world, parents are more important than ever. There is opportunity in this seemingly critical moment, but to seize it will require a new breed of parent—one capable of more than just educating and vaccinating. More than just being great, this new breed of parent will require an *extreme* parenting skill set including awareness, reason, intelligence, and strategic planning—all the necessary ingredients for turning dictatorships into sustainable relationships with their children.

Make no mistake about it, in today's world, parents are more important than ever.

Parents have not become obsolete; parents will have to learn how to compete with other influences. Raising children who are no longer oppressed by the limitations of the adults-in-charge will require the same adaptation. And just as parents of previous generations wanted to give things they never got, like new bikes for Christmas, dental care, or a college education, this is our chance to give our children crucial gifts in the form of guidance to foster relationships and build the resilience necessary to thrive in the future. No one has a crystal ball to predict the future, but we certainly can't ignore the warning signs or the incredible opportunities to shape it. So let's get started.

CHAPTER 3

Meet the Wikis

*Evolutionary memo: there is "strong," and
there is "twenty-first century strong."*

AMERICA IS PERFECTLY POISED TO reap the benefit of synergy between longevity and a coming surge of youth. Capitalizing on the synergy of wisdom and youthful aspirations can produce new ways of living and relating to each other. Whether our youth are prepared for the challenge of a new frontier will, for many, be decided in our families.

Producing a prototype always helps people understand and engage in bold ideas, so in that spirit, let's consider the ideal: a wiki. A *wiki* is a collaborative software database for creating, browsing, and searching through information with ease, seeking to update the landscape for users.

Move over, Fred Flintstone and George Jetson. There's a new family in town: the Wikis. They offer an alternative vision to our current perspective on raising kids, the role we play in their lives, and ultimately, the role they play in ours. Fortunately, the Wiki family got the evolutionary memo.

As parents, not only do Mr. and Mrs. Wiki understand, they also personify and accept their mission. They are creating an application within the family—a *wiki* (Hawaiian for "super-fast.") It's a platform designed to handle speed and unleash the entire family's potential—even the pets! Creation and collaboration replace punishment and domination.

Mr. and Mrs. Wiki are well aware that they are in charge of a complex system. In order for it to function, as well as evolve, its capacity to process information must be increased. The system must be able to identify weaknesses and bottlenecks and provide interpersonal tools in the moment that will serve for a lifetime. At the same time, Mr. and Mrs. Wiki will become adept at using chaos, control, creativity, and consistency as collective ingredients in their parenting process.

Mr. and Mrs. Wiki will work toward influencing their children, not dominating them. They will not wring their hands about control, power, or who is bigger than whom. They have decided that it is not obedience or compliance that they seek. Empathy, judgment, courage, connection, reflection, and accountability are the core elements that are being fostered. The family power will reside in self-knowledge and self-limits. Their emphasis on adaptability, resilience, and regard for all family members will remain strong. They will know that what their children believe ultimately will determine how they behave.

Striving continually to set the stage for success, Mr. and Mrs. Wiki never squander opportunities for growth by imposing aimless punitive measures. Familiar with the early indicators of what future success will look and feel like, the Wikis provide a foundation that not only serves the children but makes reasonable demands on them. They are keenly aware that they are moving toward an unknown future, but it is one that they know will certainly require more mental effort than physical brawn. It is a coordinated effort to build a child's vision of himself, one that is technically no different than those held by our founding fathers that launched us to the moon or that supported the creation of the information highway.

CHAPTER 4

Basics for Twenty-First Century Strong

PARENTS ARE THE GATEKEEPERS. MOST of us know that old-style parenting methods are failing children. A fence around the backyard offers feeble protection from the onslaught of twenty-first century menaces. Minus physical boundaries and a locked front door, the pursuit by others to hijack the hearts and minds of our children is relentless. Danger that previously could only affect a child through physical intervention, such as a visit to a "bad neighborhood," now resides in your child's bedroom! Strong gatekeeping gives kids confidence and enables their feeling of security to grow. The chance to feel safely loved and securely supported is like oxygen to their psychological development. Whether fending off a pedophile disguised as a sixth-grade teacher or "neuro-marketers" strategizing to brainwash them to crave junk food, children need us to build big psychological "keep out" signs, especially while their minds are under construction. Treat that remote and the mouse like keys to the car: no access before training, and then access only with permission.

THINK IN THE FUTURE ... ACT IN THE NOW

It is a big dilemma for all parents. In a world of countless questionable influences, when kids need us the most they will seek us out the least. This is a well-known phenomenon, especially among older kids. Parents must think beyond the measures of "good kid, bad kid." For example, even if shaming your child in response to inappropriate behavior seems to work immediately, the approach will poison your child's future. Young adults who anticipate awful feelings of shame are most at risk for self-destructive behaviors. Ask yourself, "Is what I'm doing on a consistent basis just good for the moment? Will it scale over a lifetime?" If not, you are wasting precious time.

KEEP IT REAL

The adults who were portrayed as ideal parents in popular old shows like *Father Knows Best* would probably be cast today in a show called *Father Knows Nothing*. Today's media positions children with inflated power. This is not by accident. Marketers love this formula because it directly translates into purchasing power. The more powerfully kids are portrayed in the media, the flatter the hierarchy at home, and the more likely kids will call the shots. Don't feel defeated, and don't be fooled. If you can't beat the media, then use it to your advantage.

Use the media as a tool. It is chock full of "real" lessons that would have once been considered jarring but are now just part of life. Start an ongoing conversation that keeps you real and in the game. Remember, it is never possible to always know what to do, but it is entirely possible to always know *what not to do*. Teaching your kids the difference is critical, not only for success but for their survival.

BE A LEADER, NOT A DICTATOR

It is easy to confuse the traits of leader and dictator, and it's important to realize the critical difference between the two. Leaders understand others' motivations and needs and are able to persuade and influence people over time. Dictators have no such luck. Dictators dominate to avoid being perceived as weak. They rely on power imbalances and foster fear in those around them. Don't confuse taking the time to build relationships as being weak. Your relationships with your children are the only things that will stand between them and the host of predatory influences they will encounter as their lives unfold. Parents who foster fear in their children aren't building relationships; they are destroying them. In the process, they risk losing their ability to influence during times when the stakes are high. Your job is to build a strong relationship, lead by example, and anchor your child with a consistent vision that enables growth.

CHAPTER 5

Let's Face It: Facebook is No Substitute for Face to Face

RIGHT OUT OF THE GATE, the idea of social networking had us all mesmerized by the prospect of being connected in a digital "Kumbaya." Parents made sure their kids became computer literate, horrified to think what would happen if they did not participate to the fullest in the digital age. Great idea, but bad timing.

Take a moment to stop and listen to the digital chatter. Social media will not give rise to social literacy; on the contrary, in the absence of successful face-to-face communication and relationships, it encourages social *illiteracy*.

Teens who are "hyper-networked" are at a much higher risk for stress, depression, suicide, poor academics and loss of sleep. It's not a big stretch to see how responding to more than 100 inconsequential requests a day could fragment your attention span and prevent you from learning how to really *think* about anything.

In theory, Facebook could be a good thing for kids. More social connections could lead to better communication and social skills, right? Kids would enjoy a bonanza of self-esteem and at the same time build an identity among like-minded peers that would flourish online as well as offline.

If you think that sounds too good to be true, you are right. The "wow" of social media for a young mind is very potent, just like the rush of any milestone in life. Remember walking up the street without an adult for the first time, taking training wheels off a bike or getting behind the wheel of a car without a copilot? All are experiences that carry huge boosts for maturity and self-esteem. Unfortunately, socializing online does not offer the same benefits; in fact, it inhibits them.

The hyper-networked "digital keg party" is awash with profanity-filled, narcissistic dead ends for many teens who are already in high gear and driven by emotional signals. Online communication not only amplifies emotions, it dangerously distorts them as well. Clear-headed thinking has no chance in that environment.

FEEL NO PERSON/SEE NO PERSON/HEAR NO PERSON

The verdict is in. Humans are designed to rely heavily on nonverbal input. You know that tone of voice that sounds like nails on a chalkboard, the furrowed brow that leaves "angry" lines between our eyes, or the wide-eyed look that conveys disbelief or fear? They all are a vital part of the conversation. They pace our responses to allow for reflection on both sides. Kids who are denied these face-to-face experiences early on quickly become numb to their own feelings and, even worse, become desensitized to the cues of others. A young person habituated to forming relationships primarily in this way will be left feeling intense isolation with an inability to empathize that is normally reserved for those with mental illness.

Nonverbal signals cue another person into how we are feeling or how we might react to what is being said. Face to face social feedback is critical to fostering growth and self-expression for a child. It is a continual live feed of interpersonal information indicating success or failure, connection or opposition to what the child is trying to communicate.

Without the other person's nonverbal cues, an out-of-control emotional impulse may be in the driver's seat. Tweets, e-mails and Facebooking all become weapons of personal and interpersonal destruction. Using words as sledgehammers becomes not only what *tweens* do, but all they know how to do with regard to expressing themselves. Communication, especially in a heated exchange, quickly turns verbally violent.

PARENTS IN THE DIGITAL KNOW

So how do we keep our kids socially smart? First and foremost, we have to ask the right questions. "Should my kids be allowed to partake in social networking?" poses a false choice. It is a little like asking, "Should I talk to my kids about sex?" You should. Of course you don't have to. They'll figure it out. Animals in the wild figure it out. The same goes for social media. Your kids will find their way to social networking. The real issue is addressing how their online interaction impacts their overall well-being. So ditch the question that asks, "Should I allow them on Facebook or Twitter?" and replace it with, "Am I preparing them for social media's eventual mutations?" and "Is it possible to make them smart from the start?"

It's a fact: good, regulated interpersonal communication is rewarding. A child who is raised in an environment where what he says verbally and nonverbally is acknowledged and valued will learn to do the same for others.

1. Actively engage children in face-to-face communication on a regular basis. Live, social interaction builds an interpersonal grid and provides them with lifelong capabilities of receiving and delivering information without being washed out by their own emotional undertow.

2. Be vigilant with young kids. Adopt a zero tolerance policy for verbal bombs and sledgehammers. Anonymity online encourages a "Wild West" mentality. Hold them accountable for what they say and how they say it; doing so will create a measure of accountability offline that will impact online behaviors.

Think back. Driver education did not exist before cars, right? Cars don't cause teens to crash; it is how they drive. The same story is unfolding on monitors and touch screens everywhere. Technology isn't the problem; how we use it makes all the difference. We must face the fact that it is our responsibility to teach kids how to use technology responsibly so they can hit the city streets of broadband safely.

Your update has begun.

II. AGES AND OPPORTUNITIES

INTRODUCTION:
AGES AND OPPORTUNITIES

Hope is not a plan.

Ever wonder why humans have such an extended stay in the nest? Offspring of other animals quickly reach maturity and "move out." There is minimal influence or guidance from their parents for anything beyond physical survival. That parenting playbook amounts to a short tutorial that would sound something like this: "Listen up kids: This is what you eat. This is what you drink. Stay away from any animal bigger or faster than you, and don't eat things that smell bad! Good luck!"

Despite the fact that all species are invested in the survival of their offspring, the human journey could not be more different. A child's stay in the nest is much longer than other species because the maturation process is so much more complex.

There are the obvious physical changes related to growth and development: arms and legs grow, teeth appear, and hormones start pumping. These physical processes happen with or without parental permission. And to a large degree, they happen regardless of parental involvement.

But physical maturity is not what separates us from the rest of the animal kingdom. It is our psychological and mental abilities that separate the baby boys from the baby chimps. Our abilities to change our circumstances, use tools, adapt, share ideas, and relate to each other are what earn us the title of Homo sapiens, which literally means "wise" or "knowing" man. With each successive generation, we must defend that title by doing better with what we know.

At the dawn of the twenty-first century, the research once saved for the halls of ivory towers is now going mainstream. Decades of ongoing studies have produced a wealth of compelling evidence that what happens in childhood does not stay in childhood.

In the past, raising kids was guided more by the calendar than developmental understanding. For decades, it was assumed that children who were "school-age" were "school ready." We now know that a child being of a certain age does not guarantee that emotional, cognitive, and behavioral milestones have been met, let alone mastered. Research reveals that the better we are at intervening at earlier stages to address troubling behaviors, the more likely we are to stop things from getting not only worse, but out of control. Developmental stages must be thought of more as "opportunities" than "givens."

Opportunities are not a guarantee of skills acquisition; they are simply fertile ground for acquiring them. The reality is that children are going to move through developmental stages with or without their parents' participation. For example, a child will learn to eat solid food; she may not do it with acceptable table manners, but it will happen. Children will retrieve toys from playmates. Whether it happens by force or friendlier means depends on parents' participation.

A better understanding of our children's development will maximize our opportunities with them. It is time to get beyond the notion of just stopping bad behavior. At various stages of development there are opportunities to prepare them to adapt and respond to nuance and complexity, which is the hallmark of intelligence.

It is well documented that challenges that emerge during adolescence and young adulthood have signature beginnings during childhood; how they unfold depends largely on how the hurdles are processed during those earlier years.

Children rely on previous experiences to either propel them forward or render them unable to cope with developmental challenges. Issues that go unrecognized or unaddressed can create overwhelming stress, leaving a child vulnerable to adopting destructive coping mechanisms. Over time, a lack of coping mechanisms is the precursor to greater threats, such as illegal substance or alcohol abuse, eating disorders, cutting, and anxiety. Hoping that developmental issues resolve themselves is not a plan. They are much more likely to be conquered by prevention and early intervention.

Where are the opportunities, and how do we seize them?

In a society hyper-focused on economic measures of success, parents can often focus on the wrong things, even when asking the right questions. We all are asking: Will my children be successful? Will they make good choices and have resilience? Do they have the savvy to navigate what the future holds? Will they be happy? Many assume that if we simply keep the bad stuff away and immerse children in positive activities, true champions will emerge. I call that "wishful non-thinking." What we need is a plan.

CHAPTER 6

Brain Basics

Learning is happening all the time

A MODERN UNDERSTANDING OF CHILDHOOD development would be incomplete without some basic knowledge of neurodevelopment. Increasingly, we have more information on how the brain develops and its implications for children's ultimate success.

Not long ago it was standard operating procedure to assume that a child would outgrow certain behaviors or quirks, and in some cases, behavioral issues do resolve themselves. In the majority, however, they will not. Brain maturity begs for environmental input for optimal outcome.

Knowing how your brain works is vastly different from understanding what it can do. While the brain's absolute potential still remains a mystery, we do have a fundamental understanding of how the brain matures.

We all know that it is difficult to control or influence things that we don't understand. If you do not understand the building process, you will not know how to fix your home if it falls apart. Similarly, in the absence of knowledge of a child's basic neurodevelopment, a parent can misunderstand a child's behavior and miss an opportunity to constructively address it.

We will focus on four areas that have significant impact during childhood development.

1. BE THE RESOURCE, NOT THE ENEMY

The human brain is the original search optimization engine. It has an amazing capability over time to sort through experiences and recognize patterns, making us anticipatory learners who use past experiences to predict new ones. Designed to maximize mental energy, this neurological backstop keeps us from reinventing the wheel every day.

The same brain that serves as a great mechanism for locking in the ABCs early on can lock out a parent during the teenage years. Just as Google locks in on the most frequently searched sites, your child's mind will lock onto the most frequent reactions from parents during early and middle childhood years. They develop an algorithm or shorthand for who you are and what to expect.

The critical question is, *Will you be identified as a resource or an enemy?*

For example, parents who "freak out" over spilled milk will have difficulty selling themselves as calm, cool, and collected resources during a personal crisis. A child will anticipate the freak-out even in the absence of the spilled milk. What they see from you now is what they will expect from you in the future. That neurological expectation will either chase them away (enemy) or bring them closer (resource).

2. ONLY THE STRONG SURVIVE

The ability to connect and integrate information has been shown to be a key contributor to optimal intelligence and success. Learning about money theoretically in school and then going to a store and actually participating in a financial transaction will increase the strength of the lesson. The impulse to play with a basketball should be integrated with language centers to ask for a turn. Over time, repeating that scenario will strengthen the child's ability to use language to address his needs rather than brute force. In turn, boundaries and friendships will flourish. Integration strengthens the connection and gives the skill memory muscle.

Problems arise when the strongest connections are counterproductive. Our neural network never sleeps. If new connections are not being made, then existing ones are reinforced. When the wrong connections are reinforced, they can become a block rather than a bridge to new possibilities.

While we know that many aspects of intelligence are trainable, they are also time critical. Studies of the brain activity of a professional musician whose training started before age eleven showed significantly more developed connections than those who started regular practice later in life.[1] Learning a foreign language shows similar time-critical patterns and declines after a certain age in some cases.

Researchers have identified a protein dubbed "nogo" that signals the time is up for strengthening connections in certain brain regions.[1] In other words: it's time to move on; the cake is already baked. Even in the face of recent headlines that tout lifelong brain building, it is clear that the early years provide a biological efficiency that should not be overlooked. Language, empathy, impulse control, goal setting, and perseverance are just a few of the skills that must get a head start if we want them to stick for life. The most effective way that children can reach for the stars is for parents to help them build the right connections!

---

1   R. Douglas Fields, "White Matter Matters," *Scientific American,* March 2008, accessed May 7, 2012, http://www.scientificamerican.com/article.cfm?id=white-matter-matters.

3. THINK AND LINK

In a world that spins faster by the day, thinking through action or inaction could be the difference between achieving dreams or disaster. Quick, short-term thinking has become a toxic element in all our lives. It plays itself out in everything from political gridlock and financial bubbles to a faltering education system. Wants in the short term can too easily trump longer-term needs.

Every invention or innovation, from the can opener to the television, started with a thought before it became reality. Human beings are uniquely equipped to simulate outcome in our minds. Simulation allows us to give our ideas a test run before we say yes and risk making a mess. It is a decisive skill that is too often underutilized in an increasingly complex world.

Parents are on the front line to cultivate their children's ability to simulate. They are well positioned to help them examine how their lives impact the lives of others in a deliberate and meaningful way.

The mental ability to work with information, and move forward in a constructive manner, is a core competency that begins in the home. Everything from sibling squabbles to the local science fair is a training ground. We can amplify our children's ability to think about not only the first bounce of the ball but also, in a hyper-connected world, where the ninth and tenth bounces will eventually take us. Neurological simulation enables us to enhance possibility rather than leave outcomes to chance.

If these opportunities are missed, we face the challenge of unlearning as well as relearning. Genetic preprogramming will determine exactly when the opportunities will appear. But it is the job of Mom, Dad, and educators to provide experiences through instruction and rehearsal to assure optimal development.

4. APOCALYPSE NOW ... AND LATER

As anyone who has experienced an extreme home renovation can tell you, "protect and fortify" anything that you want to keep intact while the construction crew makes room for the new addition. If support beams are not well marked, they may not survive the wrecking ball.

Raising resilient children has its own neurological version of an extreme makeover. In research circles, it is often referred to as a neurological "pruning," conjuring images of the brain being perfectly reshaped like the landscaping at Disney World. In reality, it can look and feel more like an apocalypse in the brain, a genetically preprogrammed onslaught of electrical and chemical changes that are necessary for neurological maturity. For as far back as we know, these upheavals that occur at approximately three years and thirteen years of age have existed to ensure our survival at home and out on the range.

It is well established that the storm of neurological activity that occurs in early childhood liberates children physically from their caretakers. The initial upheaval is a neurological departure from previous physical dependencies. Orchestrated by nature, the heightened activity produces little overachievers who will fall, babble, grab, and grunt until the toddler milestone work is done. Pediatricians and preschool teachers are all well trained to measure, encourage, and modify the progress.

The new circuitry that will eventually allow for running and tying shoes is initially unstable and inefficient. New and improved activities, like drinking from a cup or using utensils, eventually become second nature. Mother Nature planned it that way. Imagine having to really put mental effort into walking, working the remote, or spelling your name!

It is tough to override the efficient footprint of existing neurological connections. Ever try to forget how to tie your shoe, speak your native language, or drive a car? It is virtually impossible. The connections are strengthened every time you engage in the activity.

As an added measure during early development, to ensure a parent's directives are not usurped by peer pressures, kids enjoy being blissfully unaware. For example, their lack of self-consciousness enables them to publically wear Halloween garb in mid-July. This is an advantage for parental influence, because kids aren't as susceptible to peer review.

My advice is to nail down as many cognitive abilities as possible while you are the unchallenged influence in your child's life, before the pending apocalypse! Their neurological *inability* to gauge what other people think of them gives parents plenty of openings to steer them in the right direction. Coordinating that influence before launch is the challenge. Many of us don't look at the playbook until the fourth quarter of childhood, long after the window of opportunity has been lost.

Understanding even just the basics of adolescent development can dramatically alter how we prepare a child during middle childhood. Anticipating the second pre-programmed upheaval of neurological activity is pivotal. A physical, mental, and emotional event that says "out with the unused circuitry and in with the new" certainly should give us pause to lean into their future and really look at what they are packing psychologically for the trip.

It is important to keep in mind that the ups and downs of adolescence are a call to maturity. The whole process strikes a grand neurological bargain with your child's abilities that says, "If you use me, I will come forward with you!" It is a deliberate, decisive training ground for what to bring into adulthood and what to leave home. It is the job of parents and invested adults to ensure that they pack more than "happy" or "smart" in their duffel bag as they move away from the nest.

∽

How we guide these core processes will either expand or constrict a child's potential. Becoming familiar with some basics about brain development helps all parents become more confident, provide a better sense of what is happening, and decide where they need to go in guiding their children.

CHAPTER 7

Development Playbook: Twenty-First Century Edition

All time is not the same in child development.

THE TWENTY-FIRST CENTURY EDITION OF childhood development will cast a much wider net than becoming a superior parent. We will pick up where Dr. Spock left off. In his best-selling book, *Baby and Childcare,* Spock gave millions of mothers permission to respond in flexible ways with their children. With that same spirit, and in collaboration with nature, we will look to produce strength in places where we did not know our children had the capacity to build. What follows will go beyond the conversation of "good mom, bad mom."

Technology and research have allowed us to peer into the gestation of a fetus in the womb. We can observe this period of time dedicated to readiness. It involves the interplay of genes and environment as they unfold into mature infants ready to take on the physical world. If all goes well, the basic survival mechanisms, such as breathing, sucking, vision, motor control, and crawling, come online. In many, if not all, instances, just the watchful eye of a loving, attentive caregiver will get the job done.

It is more difficult to measure the gestation of a child's *mind,* the development and integration of mental and emotional capacities that will guide a child when beyond a parent's reach. Immature minds face a high-stake struggle in our complex world.

Development during early and middle childhood carries great opportunities. For reasons we will now explore, logic, more than science, makes the call. Front-loaded investments in early and middle childhood can have huge payoffs during those tumultuous teenage years.

THE NEW DEAL

Armed with a basic understanding of the science of neurological activity during childhood, we can move to incorporate some logic that convinces and compels. Logic is a leading factor in our "new math" of parenting. We reach way beyond "because I said so" and challenge the illogic of being smacked for hitting your brother. Development guided by logic delivers a new deal that requires parents to lean into their child's future. Many elite athletes know the drill well. Hockey greats, hall-of-fame quarterbacks, and other star athletes all follow the rule. Wayne Gretzky famously said, "I don't skate to the puck; I skate to where the puck will be." Any competent quarterback knows that you don't target the receiver; you target where he will be. It is that unique ability to calculate and lean into the motion that separates the champions from the players. In parenting parlance, it is the difference between having babies and raising kids. The more predictable and responsive we are as caregivers, the better prepared they will be to predict and respond to their world.

REAPING WHAT YOU SOW

Once the initial dots to the future are connected, the learning curve is greatly reduced. Principles that do not shift with the wind can be instilled and operational for use over a lifetime.

Moving from diapers to the toilet and from eating with hands to using utensils are good examples of progression toward an almost-guaranteed goal. It is the next dimension of challenge that leaps from using the toilet to cleaning the bathroom, or from eating a meal to cleaning up afterward, that is on shaky ground. Taking on those unguaranteed goals with equal verve is more important than ever.

The added dimensions are desirable, certainly not necessary, and in no way guaranteed. The world will continue to turn with a dirty toilet or dishes in the sink. That is not the issue. Dirty dishes are not just dirty dishes; they are an obstacle to your next meal. They represent a basic lack of accountability or foresight for what happens next. An aware parent can plant the seeds for accountability or foresight on a larger scale right next to her child's bowl of Fruit Loops or plate of pasta.

PARENTING: DON'T LEAVE HOME WITHOUT IT

My clinical experience has made it very apparent that fostering certain traits and skills in children is much more efficient at certain stages than others. Missing these windows of opportunity can lead to the frustration of helplessly witnessing your child fail to meet her potential. The conventional folk wisdom passed down through generations is not going to save her; instead, a solid foundation of skills and attitudes will be the prevention and, in some cases, the cure.

Around twelve years of age, mental habits, belief systems, capabilities, and signs of corruption will all begin to surface for one last tweak. Soon your child will turn into a teenager and your influence will become greatly reduced. Incorporating the following core elements will make that transition far more functional and far less scary for all involved.

Three "must-have" principles are necessary at every turn ahead. They are the "American Express of parenting": no one should leave the delivery room without them.

1. OPERATE FROM THE SAME PLAYBOOK

All too often, parents dive into parenting with a laundry list of vague goals. I have engaged hundreds of parents to compare their lists with their partners, and rarely do we have an exact match. Worse yet, when asked how they will attain those goals, the page remains blank. When parents do not operate from the same playbook, they lose. Sending a mixed message to your kids is worse than sending no message at all. And it essentially defines parents as the Keystone Cops and causes children to lose confidence in their authority. A professional sports team would never approach a game without a shared playbook. Neither should you!

2. KNOW YOUR END GAME

Many parents rush into situations without any sense of what they want to accomplish. I often challenge them by asking, "Would you attend a business meeting without a plan?" or "Would you ever go for a haircut and not have an expected outcome?" Never! Then why do we permit ourselves to barrel into transactions with our children without a clear set of objectives? Because too often we don't know what is possible in the moment or how to attain it. Just that simple acknowledgement solves half the problem. The other half is to create a plan.

3. CONSISTENCY CREATES CREDIBILITY

Parents who are inconsistent with their children lose credibility.

There will come a time when you are restricted to only being able to predict the future for your child. For example, predicting that if the dishwasher is not emptied, there will be no access to video games later that evening. How parents have conducted themselves from day one in terms of follow-through is critically important in the later years. Credibility does not happen overnight; it happens over a decade. A teen will be much more likely to heed a message about not texting while driving from parents who have consistently refrained from that behavior themselves. They will also be more apt to comply with curfews at sixteen if they were properly enforced during play dates at age six.

Parents who use these must-haves will more likely cultivate a secure atmosphere for their kids, one that will leave them freer to grow knowing that thoughtful, strategic adults are providing the groundwork for their futures.

Remember that the level of exposure or engagement necessary to influence a child will differ, and it is never too late to begin.

COUNTDOWN TO LAUNCH
Ages 0–3 Years
Opportunity: Build a Foundation for Self-Regulation

Little Einsteins. In recent years, media messages touting the development of baby geniuses have flooded parents with misinformation. It is a marketing message that is pointing parents in the wrong direction and needs to be put aside.

The truth is, an infant's brain is not designed to process cognitive input. Their senses serve as windows to the world, capturing signals and creating responses that foster relationships with their surroundings.

Several decades of research reveals that the bonding that occurs during the first years of life creates critical underpinnings for the child's emotional well-being. At the mercy of their uncoordinated nervous systems, infants and toddlers depend on our responses to help them. The more predictable and responsive we are as caregivers, the better prepared our children will be to predict and respond to the world. Resist the frenzy to foster Mozart or encourage an Einstein with countless drills, classes, seminars, and videos that tax both children and parents. Our job is to reduce stress, not create it.

As caregivers respond to children in a nurturing manner, the children learn to seek comfort through relationships. It is a template that will serve them throughout their development, participating in the ebb and flow of behaviors that draw people to them. In turn, they have the opportunity to foster security through connection. Feelings of reward for cooperating emotionally with their caregivers are the beginnings of children being able to regulate themselves. It is their first step toward *pro-social* empathic behaviors. The less experience they have with regulation, the less opportunity for children to develop neurological connections that stop emotional outbursts. Without those connections, they are more likely to develop reduced thresholds for stress that can easily manifest in anxiety, explosiveness, learning issues, and relationship problems later in life.

The ability to self-regulate has been correlated to everything from resilience and empathy to higher-order thinking, creativity, successful relationships, and problem solving. Without being able to self-regulate, there is no chance of constructively influencing your environment.

Informed, conscious interaction with a caregiver or parent is the most powerful way to ensure that a baby starts this process early in life. Investing in and strengthening this ability in your child from day one will have a huge payoff.

Caregivers and parents need to be aware that, prior to the ability to use language, a child is remarkably attuned to absorbing sensory information from his environments, including your voice, face, touch, tone, and movement. They all impact your child whether you are interacting directly with him or having a fight with your spouse. The messages cascading into his nervous system are making a permanent record, forming custom physiological connections that create an emotional highway of information between you and your child. Over time, that input determines whether your child's system will be able to connect to others and learn, or be at the mercy of its own immaturity.

Stable, predictable caregiving that avoids emotional landmines will give your child the best chance for developing emotional regulation. Parents who struggle with their own control are downloading an amplified emotional response into their child's system. Depending on the child's natural temperament, this could either encourage her to shut down or prime her to be explosive herself.

The real difficulty is that you won't know the impact until later when challenges in development surface. Responses that were downloaded prior to development of language will make them exceptionally difficult to modify and control.

What You Should Do

Infants and toddlers cannot tell you what is happening to them. Many parents are blindsided by how difficult it is to keep their cool in the face of an unruly infant or toddler. Unprepared, caregivers allow their systems to go haywire and in turn amplify the cycle of blown emotional circuits with their children.

From day one, being responsive and well regulated yourself is critical. Become aware of your own physiology. Know the warning signs that you are about to overheat. Breathe. If you are not able to respond constructively, either get help or get out of the room. Collect yourself and begin again.

3–7 Years

<u>Opportunity</u>: *Beginnings of Independence and Pro-social Behaviors*

Before you know it, your child will be launched into the digital world of "do as you please," a potential communication wasteland where regard for others is nonexistent. Never before has it been as critical as it is now to make sure that children use language to connect. Every experience from the first "Mamma" or "Dadda" should reinforce connection.

Language is a pivotal factor in everything from impulse control to executive functioning in young and old alike. How we speak is linked to how we think and therefore to how we act. Family culture builds the template for language. Once kids reach physical independence from parents, your authority will rely heavily on language-based communication. Scooping up a child from a problematic situation will give way to verbal directives, such as "Look both ways" or "Please let your sister join the game."

So much of a person's life depends on language skills. An unsuspecting child can use them to preserve dignity or take it away. Children who are allowed to habitually bark commands or name call miss opportunities to send signals that foster connection and reflection.

A constant chorus from parents is that children don't "respect" them. Kids who live on a steady diet of "No," "Shut up," "I hate you," or "Get out of here" have little likelihood of responding in a respectful way, even if they respect the person they are addressing. Parents can easily lose their cool when children speak as though they are thumbing their noses at them.

My first thought is, "Do the children possess the language necessary to convey respect?" Unfortunately, most parents don't model language that helps children build relationships, show respect, or solve problems. In turn, they become very upset when a child comes up short with a retort of "Get out of here" instead of "May I have privacy, please?" Parents must consider the consequences of the language they model when their children boomerang the habit back to them. Think of what you want to hear from your child, and use that language. It is vitally important to interact with youngsters in a way that acknowledges regard for others; it is key to positive constructive outcomes.

Language-based acknowledgements and connectors are critical building blocks. They are the precursors for acquiring vital communication skills and setting boundaries later in development. For example, it is completely possible to expand a four- or five-year-old's language skill from "I'm thirsty" to "Mom, may I have some milk, please?" A six- or seven-year-old is capable of acknowledging a rule and requesting an exception. For example, instead of "I hate you" as a response to a bedtime directive, a parent might hear, "Dad, I know it is bedtime, but would it be okay if we finished?" which opens up a whole new world for you and your kids.

Use language that connects. Simple phrases, such as "I see you are busy" or "I know we are in a rush," convey regard for others. They are powerful seeds to good early language habits that create connections instead of dead ends.

Golden Boundaries

Good boundaries are the first step in living the Golden Rule. Morality, generosity, cooperativeness, and mutual respect are all born of *Do unto others as you would have them do unto you.*

It is in their early social experiences that children learn where they end and where others begin. As the world opens up beyond Mom and Dad, playmates and play dates provide the building blocks of healthy boundaries with others.

The key is to provide the structure so that the right things are reinforced, and the wrong things are avoided or eliminated. Caregivers need to *supervise at a distance where they can intervene* if necessary.

Too often, kids are left to their own devices early on, with parents thinking they will work social situations out on their own. *They will not.* Play dates that follow parental hands-off policies foster mayhem. Four-year-old children without supervision are the blind leading the blind. Those encounters only reinforce the bad stuff and sometimes block the good.

The alternative is setting kids up for success by providing them with expectations, rules, and the necessary level of monitoring to achieve them.

Unfortunately, many caregivers go into situations arming small kids only with a reactive directive to "be nice." What many don't realize is that the primitive behaviors children engage in actually often *do feel nice* to them. Biting or backhanding for a toy can have a huge payoff. They have no concept of the impact they are having on others; that's what they need to be taught. Especially in situations where willful children dominate the group, intervention is a must. All kids at this age use certain behaviors because they don't have an alternative script. They must be redirected and given examples of productive language and behaviors. Give them guidance, and make sure you are around to see the behavior unfold properly. Confirmation from an adult adds clarity to the directive and boosts the child's learning.

Behavioral science shows that reinforcing behavior that elicits trust will in turn engender trust. For freewheeling four-year-olds, that means playtime *according to the rules* will be contagious. Playmates who use hands for helping and not hitting will become early adaptors and trendsetters for the group. Their habits will promote pro-social behaviors among their peers that enable kids to gain intrinsic rewards from doing the right thing. Once this feedback loop is in place, the wrong behaviors will rarely show up.

Foster Responsibility, Not Blame

"Who did what to whom?" is the $64,000 question in most households with young kids. Kids can be quick to blame others to avoid feeling bad themselves, even though they know they are wrong. It is a pattern that can infiltrate every relationship in their lives. As the saying goes, it is never the crime; it is the cover-up. Inability to own one's behavior can become a real barrier to personal reflection and growth over a lifetime.

Beware of developing patterns where taking responsibility is equated to punishment. Kids, especially sensitive ones, will dig very deep holes to avoid being blamed. Loud protests and name-calling are common distractions to avoid punishment. Shift the focus to highlighting the truth regardless of fault. Even preschoolers can learn to take responsibility for their behavior if they are not under threat.

At this stage, most violations are low stakes, and every incident should be turned into a learning opportunity. Youngsters are not looking to save face; they simply want their turn or their toy.

The majority of kids are not even sure of their motivation. "Why" questions are far less productive than "what" questions. Parents should try to discover "what happened" rather than ask "why" a child did something.

Here is a sample scene on a playground: Justin is crying as he approaches an adult on duty. He indicates that John hit him while they were playing basketball.

The adult might handle the situation by scolding John for hitting, but it's a short-term solution that doesn't reveal the truth of the matter. Take the time to get the facts. Give them space to tell the truth and address the situation accordingly, as in this example:

Adult: "John, what happened before you hit Justin?"

John: "Justin wouldn't give me a turn."

Adult: "Justin, did you give John his turn?"

Justin: "No."

Adult: "John, did you hit Justin to get a turn?"

John: "Yes."

Adult: "Justin, if you can't take turns, you will not be able to play. Are you able to take turns?"

Justin: "Yes."

Adult: "John, hitting doesn't solve the problem; getting help from an adult does."

An exchange of apologies can reset the play clock. Always encourage young ones to value the truth and be accountable for their actions. Once kids find reward in telling the truth, they are more apt to do it.

Competence

A sense of competence is the precursor to confidence, the magic ingredient to a child's sense of self. Eager to help our kids attain success, we can unintentionally block their ability to create this magic. In a world that delivers ease and parents who are eager to please, kids can be robbed of opportunities to develop their own senses of competence and self-reliance. Think big, and start small. Always look for "just right" challenges to enhance a child's sense of industry. So much of how our daily lives unfold is invisible to children. Learning how to fold laundry or prepare a sandwich goes a long way in demystifying how the world works.

Kids may not come with instructions, but they certainly need them. Life is so hectic that it might seem easier *for you* in the short run to fold their clothes or put on their shoes, but consider whether that will make life harder *for them* in the long run.

This is the time to plant the seeds of competence and confidence that will help them grow throughout their lives.

Beware of "Techno-Creep"

The long-time concern about kids watching too much TV has evolved to staggering proportions, thanks to a deluge of screen time available in multiple formats anytime, anywhere. Parents on the go can be caught off guard by how dramatically their child's viewing habits can increase. In turn, precious developmental space is being diverted to passive isolating activities that do nothing to prepare them for effortful learning.

At one time, the content of contemporary media was the main concern expressed by experts. And although the jury is still out on to what degree content matters, that concern is now dwarfed by a bigger concern: the effect of passively watching a screen. Given what we know about healthy brain development, it's not surprising that young children are particularly vulnerable to the negative impact of long-term screen time.

We know that stimulation of higher brain regions occurs through sensory input. Unfortunately, the children's programming crafted by marketing professionals offers screen time that provides the opposite effect. The never-ending stream of amusement puts a child's mind in a hypnotic state, muting these very important connections.

Habituating to this state can easily become the norm. It is the antithesis of effortful learning and can impact the way children participate in the world, as passive viewers. Over time, actual living, such as putting on their shoes, getting up to answer the doorbell, or coming into the kitchen for dinner, can seem like too much work. Draw the line, and stop the techno-creep. Technology should and will be integrated into every aspect of their lives, but not at the expense of all other experiences and learning opportunities. Remember, kids have no idea of the power or reward in real-world learning. This age is the perfect time to feed their appetites for real-world experiences that free them from a screen that does the thinking for them!

7–11 Years

Opportunity: *Shape Beliefs, Flexible Thinking, and Accountability*

Waste not; want not. Invested, involved parents continue to have enormous cachet at this stage, while their children's foundations are still under construction. Kids remain accessible, and the stakes are still fairly low. This is probably a parent's last opportunity to interact and have influence without much interference from the high drama often caused by biological or environmental factors associated with tweens.

It is around this time that kids develop an appetite for separation. Our reprieve from car seats and cutting their food gives way to crises over what to wear and daily mood swings! Kids are looking not only for physical separation but also separation from their parents' ideas and beliefs. They begin to build an inner landscape of their own notions and preferences, becoming adventurous about everything from food to friends. Onetime favorites become distant memories. They will seek experiences to take their emerging new beliefs or haircuts for a test-drive and see how far they can go. They may challenge authority, eat new foods, change playmates, or ask to drop out of a former favorite activity. These are all signs of an emerging independent identity.

As new preferences and priorities simultaneously make the scene, our children are required to manage their immediate wants with future goals, all of which are just coming into awareness.

Developing a way of thinking and responding to the world constructively will impact our children on all levels. Parents also will begin to see evidence of *recursive* thinking or behaviors. These are ideas or behaviors that no longer require original stimuli to make them happen. Translation: you reap the behaviors that you sow in your children. Some of them will be desirable; some, not so much. For example, kids who were encouraged by one parent to keep information from the other will eventually withhold information on their own without being cued. And a parent that constantly offers unsolicited opinions or criticism to children runs the risk of his kids exhibiting the same behavior.

As influences and complications begin to flood children's worlds, now is the time to focus on cleaning up some of those unwanted bad habits and building a core for problem solving and self-reflection. Children with a clear internal framework for responding to a variety of situations will feel far more confident about their options in the future.

Language of Thinking

We need language to connect and coordinate with others. Simple social situations or needs don't require mastery over much more than "May I have a cookie?" or "What's your name?" or "You're annoying!"

However, this basic communication is not enough to navigate situations that involve more complex personal needs as well as the needs of others. Just as emotional intelligence has become a significant ingredient in a successful life, the ability for flexible thinking is equally important. Parents who continually resort to "do as I say" directives are blocking opportunities for their children to learn how to adapt their thinking and bolster resilience when things do not go their way.

Providing opportunities to acquire language skills that build futures requires seizing everyday opportunities and dedicated effort. The onslaught of pop language will be a formidable force for your child to resist. Using phrases like "whatever" or "I don't know" to shut down conversation absolves children of attempting to articulate not only what they want but also what is important to them. Kids must be given time and opportunity to acquire language that will enable them to be successful in cognitively demanding situations.

At this age, children are gleefully unaware of their impending appetite for the world at large. Complicated relationships, new ideas, power, independence, and self-reliance will all be eclipsing early childhood needs and awareness in the coming years.

For pre-teens, developing the ability to sort through the noise creeping into their heads and send clear signals rarely happens on its own. Strengthening the use of language to help them think through a variety of factors will require practice and support from adults.

Right now, allowing immature statements, such as "I hate school" or "You treat me like a baby," to stand as mature expression will leave your child directionless. Teach and model language that builds a bridge to their experience. Say, "Let's evaluate what you don't like about school," or encourage them to declare, "Feeling independent is important to me." Both contain the seeds of expression that will help them get what they want while revealing the people they are becoming.

The time to offer children a template to help them navigate their emotions and define their needs is while they are still a captive audience. Learning to use language to express thoughts and influence their environment will give them the confidence necessary to reflect more complicated selves. Eventually they will be called upon to clarify their ideas and evaluate a wide range of input on their own.

Processing Experiences

Years before they feel the need to "save face" in front of adults, kids can be taught to take apart situations with less emotion and minimal drama. Revisiting an event or an incident that did not end well builds the first layer of thinking beyond impulse or emotional gratification.

Our streets are littered with casualties of poor problem solving. Much of it is rooted in the inability to create a *shared understanding* about what was happening in the moment, which leads to turmoil, unproductive reactions, and unresolved problems. Kids who never develop a comfort level or sense of reward from exploring options during disagreeable events remain at very high risk for repeating mistakes throughout their lives. Now is the time to download a script that helps solve problems and avoids making them worse.

New cognitive real estate that is coming online for kids will allow them to sort out what is relevant and what is not. With practice and effort, they can move from processing small bits of information to creating real context. Blossoming language skills coupled with the desire for independence provides great motivation to think through actions, even after the fact. With help, kids can mentally take apart the events and identify the salient, important aspects of the situation. Connecting these dots with language allows kids to focus mental energy on considering alternatives.

At first, processing what happened—the good, the bad, and how they participated—can be uncomfortable. Fear of being wrong or misunderstood, or losing a privilege, can block being open to full disclosure. Creating context is how we explain ourselves and decide what moves to make. Oddly enough, revisiting the recent past helps children keep an eye on their futures.

By revisiting situations and considering alternative behaviors, kids can gain wider perceptions while seeing how to alter outcomes. Encouraging kids to process experiences from getting poor grades to peer conflict will go a long way in providing stability during the looming upheaval of adolescence. When parents take the time to direct kids in specific circumstances, they are providing building blocks of mutual understanding and cooperation.

Remember, life is becoming more complex, as it should. The initial demands of combining sensory information, emerging personal preference, and past experiences may feel like a juggling act for kids. They need opportunities to sort out complex input. Listening thoughtfully to children doesn't mean you agree with them. It gives them a level of comfort and allows them the time to craft what they think. Reexamining events from a variety of angles takes confidence that only comes from experience. Taking the time to talk through experiences provides kids a framework for sorting out the costs and benefits of their behaviors. Away from the emotional charge of the moment, kids are able to learn how to push back in a constructive way. In other words, they can articulate their objections without drama. This story illustrates how a parent can set the stage to do just that.

Articulating Objections Without Drama

It was the close of summer vacation. After a long week at the beach, nine-year-old Tyler and his family were ready to head home. They'd had a great time on vacation with friends and family, many of whom Tyler would see in the coming days when school reopened. Earlier in the day, he had asked his parents if they could make one more stop at the local toy store before getting on the road. He had his eye on a novel yo-yo that was not available at home. When he reminded his dad about the stop, the answer was, "No, there isn't enough time." Tyler could not contain his disappointment, badgering and crying in ways that completely belied his age.

Although he was getting increasingly agitated with his son's behavior, instead of adding to the fire, Tyler's dad challenged him to get a hold of himself and make at least one convincing statement about why they should stop at the store. Dad was giving him the time to be a better politician for himself. Wiping away tears and catching his breath, Tyler said, "My friends have this yo-yo and will practice all week and be better than me on the first day of school. I want it to practice."

Tyler's dad had to give pause to the enormous scale of a yo-yo in a nine-year-old boy's life. From that vantage point, Tyler's reasoning contained every lesson his dad was currently trying to instill: work at things you want in life, take responsibility for outcomes, think ahead and plan, no one else will do it for you, and stand up for yourself. Tyler's logic made his dad stand down; the yo-yo was secured, and the lesson was learned.

Just as champion athletes review tapes, parents looking to raise winners must adopt a similar mindset with their children. Awareness is central to all forms of problem solving. Take the time to review situations. Get the facts as your child sees them. Saying things out loud helps build context and create awareness that will serve them well in the coming years.

Emotional Alignment

A core tenet of mental health is the ability to recognize personal needs and have the wherewithal to achieve them. Raised on a steady diet of being "seen and not heard," large segments of our population have slipped into adulthood lacking this essential capability.

Just as all children need time and practice to coordinate their limbs before they can walk, they need practice to orchestrate balance between emotions and actions.

Even though kids may have access to everything from iPhones to iPads that serve as online megaphones for what they think and do, unless they develop a connection to what they really want or need, they are still going to be lost and misunderstood.

We know that impending neurological changes will inundate kids with more emotion and less direction for their behaviors. Putting the brakes on emotionally driven outbursts or actions will require a steady guiding hand. Unassisted, kids can create a big gap between what they need and their ability to get those needs met.

Being able to clarify their personal motivations and become aware of their impact on others are vital skills that will help close that gap. It requires going beyond metrics that measure only good or bad, right or wrong. It requires answering the question, "What are my needs?" Being able to align feeling with actions is the beginning of understanding oneself. For example, increasing anxiety can easily be misrepresented by displays of anger. A child becoming anxious about arriving on time for school can attack his "slow poke" sister without ever acknowledging his anxiety about being tardy. Anger at his sister will win far fewer fans than a plea for help with his anxiety about walking into a classroom late.

Taking the time to correct faulty assumptions not only gives kids permission to have latitude in their thinking, it allows for latitude with others. Such simple acknowledgments of self are the beginnings of self-understanding. Both are precursors to understanding of others.

Generating clarity in one's own motives builds a sense of accountability in a young mind. The early ability to articulate and move toward meeting their own needs builds a belief in themselves. It generates the kind of confidence that raises the bar high for themselves, and raises it for what they expect from others. And it's a sure way to keep them in good company.

PREPARING FOR LAUNCH INTO ADOLESCENCE AND BEYOND
11–13 Years
Opportunity: *Situational Awareness and Judgment*

Entering preadolescence carries all the harbingers of things to come. Old rules of engagement no longer apply. A child's mind is now able to see beyond the family horizon. The world according to Mom and Dad is being drowned out by peer influences and personal preferences. Preadolescents are becoming aware that they will need to adapt to new environments, from middle school to social events without adult supervision.

The windows to the world that their senses once provided are morphing into a house of mirrors. This is a time when a child shifts from outwardly declaring intentions to become everything from an astronaut to a ballerina, into total preoccupation with such things as the part in her hair. More than a journey, the odyssey of transformation begins.

Have We Met?

Kids have a new and growing appetite to take in the world that, at times, can make them seem unrecognizable to their parents. All terrain, from social situations to science class, is beginning to morph in their minds. They are having difficulty sorting out who is friend or foe. Unaware, parents can easily slip into enemy territory without knowing how they got there.

As children's perception of the world changes, what motivates them will shift as well. Many preteens seem destined to become card-carrying members of the high school drama club. Benign events that were blips on their radar screens are seen as life or death high-stakes situations.

Remember, their brains are maturing in ways that ensure their launch. All of this new high-octane fuel does have a practical and evolutionary purpose: if these internal changes did not occur, teens would never take the risk and leave their bedrooms!

Magnified emotional responses are there to ensure engagement and investment in the outside world. They provide the propulsion necessary for their launch into true adolescence and preparation for young adulthood.

Now is the time to provide mental scaffolding for a young mind, the kind of support that will foster better judgment whether your child is in the home or out in the world on his own. Staying on message and communicating well-defined expectations to kids is vitally important. Putting to use the tools practiced at earlier stages is key for them. The essential ability to sort through various incoming stimuli and evaluate situations for constructive outcomes will be invaluable in the years to come.

As parents' influence fades away, kids will need to advance the cognitive skills that are portable and reliable as their world becomes increasingly unstable. It is prime time to introduce and reinforce new layers of cognitive processes upon which children can rely wherever they go.

"E" for Effort

Nate was not in the mood to look for his baseball cleats on a cold January afternoon. On this day, the high school freshman was protesting the baseball conditioning sessions that he eagerly committed to last fall. But as often is the case, the fifteen-year-old was being led by his feelings.

His dad was not happy about the weekly pattern of complaints from his son about how he did not "feel" like going to the gym. Nate had failed to make his spring all-star team and was feeling insecure about his prospects for the baseball team tryouts. As a strategy to give him a better shot, he asked his parents if he could condition during the winter to be at his best come March. They agreed and made arrangements.

Frustrated and confused by Nate's reluctance to act on his own commitment, Nate's parents arranged a session with me to discuss their concerns. I explained that teens can easily be influenced by the power of their feelings. Combined with a new appetite for independence, they can often make short-term decisions based on feelings that undermine their own longer-term goals. We discussed how this was less about personality and more about the skill and practice necessary to push through very common initial feelings of reluctance on the way to a greater goal. We emphasized that no person who accomplished anything worthwhile "always" felt like doing the work necessary to get there. Nate was going to have to find his "push," the ability to push through his own resistance to effort. Taking charge of where the effort went was a building block in how to build his life in the future.

At home, Nate's parents sidestepped any punitive measure. Instead, they shared with him the insights about what the level of achievement he was after would require. Amenable to the logic, Nate still whined a little, but finished the program. Later in the spring, he joined the team with all the other kids who pushed themselves through winter conditioning, as a young man with a renewed sense of his capacity for effort that would serve him in all seasons of his life.

As predictable diversions come into their lives, children must find the way to push through initial feelings of ambivalence. Muscling through short-term mood shifts or distractions tests young achievers and future leaders.

Looking to remain in control or powerful when feeling increasingly overwhelmed, it is easy for kids to become uncomfortable when a challenge, academic or otherwise, requires new levels of determination, especially in the absence of immediate reward.

At this age, they are building habits that separate the "dreamers" from the "doers." The days of everybody's poem on display, the entire class appearing in the school play, or everyone making the baseball team are numbered. Once the low fruit of success is achieved, what or who makes the next cut will be based on accomplishments that require *effort*.

Knowing how to summon energy and invest it in the right direction can make or break a life.

Most kids do not yet realize that greatness doesn't come easy. With so much hype around celebrity and overnight sensations in our society, kids live off a steady narrative that neglects what real accomplishment looks or feels like.

Additionally, kids can easily be fooled by mixed emotions. Because feeling centers will be coming on strong in coming months and years, recognizing that initial feelings can be misleading is very important.

Our kids need to be reminded that worthwhile goals are rarely achieved in a straight line, and that they are seldom achieved by people who allow themselves to be directed by their moods alone. Anybody who has achieved anything worthwhile has had to push through initial feelings of procrastination or uncertainty about success. I am sure countless masterpieces never made it to the canvas because the artist failed to "feel like" doing it.

We need to give the signal that expending a certain level of effort is as important as an academic "A." It can make all the difference in how far a child will pursue her own dreams and ideas. Several studies confirm that early achievers who use little effort can become timid in the face of uncertain success, yet those who become accustomed to greater effort early on are better able to sustain levels of achievement even in the face of uncertainty. Kids must become comfortable with a sustained level of perseverance, the kind of persistence and mental muscle that pushes creative people into being creators.

If you see a pattern of your child succumbing to feelings of indifference about goals after the initial excitement wears off, he may need guidance to help him find his "push." Be ready to insist on some measure of commitment. Keep him on track to find the reward of pushing through to the pot of gold that wasn't visible at the beginning of the journey.

Tenth Bounce Thinking

As the buzzing and confusion of the real world becomes louder, kids are beginning to rely heavily on their own internal signals. Caught up in the novelty of being independent, they can easily lose their situational awareness, losing sight of the longer-reaching impact of their actions or inactions. Internet posts or pictures, unfinished school assignments, or the perennial favorite—disorganized belongings—are all just a few places where we see them lose ground.

Tweens begin to discover a newfound urgency for their own agendas. New priorities and influences quicken their pace of thinking, making them quite vulnerable to impulses and, therefore, instability. This need not be the case. Amid all of this upheaval, their minds are beginning to develop the ability to hold an idea or notion in the abstract. Consider a ball bouncing down the road. An immature mind might consider the impact of the first or second bounce because it is visible, but as a child's mind develops, she can consider its path far down the road. The same holds true about children's actions at this stage; now they are capable of considering farther-reaching implications.

For example, the thirteen-year-old who throws a tantrum while trying to convince his parents that he is mature enough to attend an R-rated movie is in dire need of situational awareness. The illogic of the moment can be unnerving to any parent. Resisting your own reactivity, show him where the ball will land. Kids will respond to a parent's latitude to regroup and rethink once the dust has cleared.

> Fresh off her sixteenth birthday, with her driver's permit in hand, Jill could not wait to make her own money and start to save for a car, so she was thrilled about her steady summer job. She would be babysitting four times a week for a local family, an opportunity that came her way due to a classmate's referral.

During the spring of her junior year, Jill was enjoying the company of her friends so much that she decided to share pictures of good times on Facebook with the world, the world that included her new employer. With a beer in one hand and a permanent marker in the other, Jill was snapped drawing on someone's face who lay sleeping on a couch. Harmless prank, right? Wrong.

Jill's new employer, a mom of three small children, saw the photo. It didn't take long for her to call and cancel the summer job. She wasn't comfortable with Jill's decision making. Jill protested and said, "I didn't do anything to her, and I wouldn't hurt the kids." It didn't matter. The woman had other child care options and said she would pass.

Jill did not think about how that photo would influence people's opinions of her. Because she was used to the cachet of good grades, being a solid athlete, and having cheerleading parents, having to accept responsibility for her identity in a fickle, competitive world was a shock to her system.

Kids on the verge of young adulthood must be crystal clear that Mom and Dad can no longer campaign for them. They must begin to govern their lives in a way that will make the world say yes to their hopes and plans. Jill had not thought of anything but the first bounce of her action. Even before the age of the Internet, winners were always the people who calculated the power and reach of how their actions or inactions would carry forward. Today, winners are still the ones who get where they want to go and don't end up forced into places other people send them ... such as the unemployment line.

Thinking in the abstract is what propelled us to the moon and put a microprocessor in everyone's pocket. At its core, that type of thinking is the same driving force behind the transition into young adulthood. The challenge is to make sure it is used.

Problem Resolving

Innovative thinking is the new smart. American dreams don't come easy. Kids don't know that over the course of a lifetime almost no one's "plan A" ever works out. Whether it is the purchase of a home or an Olympic dream, most of us are working with plan "D" or "E." Unanticipated problems surface due to limited resources or circumstances out of our control. At the same time, many have experienced satisfaction as they discover that the process of adjusting and pursuing goals in the face of challenges is very worthwhile and rewarding. Innovation thrives on the ability to maximize resources and make novel connections when the chips are down.

Even so, dreams die hard, and kids have difficulty accepting some of the limitations families face. Physical, financial, and emotional obstacles can combine to put a wrench in the best-laid plans. Being able to remain clear in the face of disappointment and generate alternatives is a priceless skill for anyone with a big appetite for success.

College rejections, athletic losses, missed job opportunities, failed romances, or erroneous financial calculations will all come knocking on your child's door at one time or another. While many parents are tempted to do the thinking for their children, that interference can often leave them feeling helpless. We mistakenly make sure they get the right answers rather than teach them how to generate alternative solutions.

Early adolescence allows them space to reevaluate situations and make something happen. By resolving problems, they can expand their sense of capability. Kids at this age need to develop intrinsic motivation to take on tasks that are difficult yet worthwhile.

Tap into your kids' budding abstract thinking and guide them to reorganize elements to create alternative solutions. Opportunities for this abound in the everyday. Managing their money toward a large purchase or making difficult social choices due to time constraints all add up to feeling in charge and in control. The ability to work within limitations and land on their feet is crucial. Reworking problems and finding new ways to reach modified goals is a *life giver* in this fast-paced world.

The Ability to Convey Import

With each passing year, tweens become animated by what is important to them. Music, politics, grades, fashion, social status, and more will all begin to emerge as having meaning in their world. The challenge comes with giving a clear voice to that meaning. As their world grows, they will encounter a variety of competing and contrasting influences for their attention and investment—from peers, parents, and people they have not even met. Fortunately, most situations at this point are low-stakes and changeable. Articulating what matters in the face of such incoming, and sometimes opposing, forces is never easy, but putting in the time to rehearse such a skill is well worth the effort. There is nothing that will raise your child's stock more quickly in this world than the ability to clearly articulate her posture on a given preference or topic. It's a skill that not only helps her carve an identity to the outside world, but it also helps her have clear "self-talk" about what is going on internally. Now is the time for her to begin building her own internal constitution not only about who she is, but who she is not!

Today, one of the biggest hindrances to kids finding their voices is "pop language," the sort of catchall phrases that tweens use to *unsuccessfully* communicate what is important to them. Standard protest lines, such as "You're a loser!" or "That teacher is a jerk!" or "You treat me like a baby!" or the most baneful of all, "Whatever!" at best plant the wrong seeds and at worst absolve our children of the responsibility of making their needs known.

Everyone needs practice if he wants to acquire the skill necessary to articulate that future fabulous idea. On the face of it, what *is* said is not much. What is *not* said is the problem. Don't let kids off the hook—insist that they clearly express their ideas while they're trying to influence you to see things their way. Direct them to put effort into articulating what they want. Ban phrases that shut down conversations. Kids grow their sense of self-worth when they have skin in the game beyond consumption and achievement. Requiring that they be responsible for conveying their ideas or protests with more than canned responses is the best way to get them there.

Cultivate Compassion

Social science informs us that human beings are designed for one-on-one empathy and compassion. Studies show that sending broad messages to "feed the hungry" can make even the most empathic adults feel overwhelmed and fatigued from compassion before they can change the channel. These big dispatches from the field are equally as overwhelming to kids. Seeing big celebrity events as the de facto way to help the needy is like asking them to run a humanitarian marathon before they can walk. We also run the risk that they will tune out similar messages for good.

There is no greater way to cultivate an adolescent child's sense of power than to provide her with an opportunity to feel her true self-worth by assisting another person in need. Working within our natural design is the only way to enlist our children's helping hands so that they may feel the rush. The key is to think local now and find opportunities to put their hands to work.

Whether we get them involved with reading to younger kids at school, volunteering at the SPCA, or collecting items for their local homeless shelter, making these connections a natural part of their identities as they craft their independent selves is vital. Comfort them with the fact that making an impact on the local level is the first step to ensuring they participate and go global later on!

CHAPTER 8

Decoding Teens

As the teenage years approach, parents may hear the music from *2001: A Space Odyssey*, its pounding drumbeat signaling that something is emerging. Late adolescence/early adulthood has long been perceived as a problem, and parents can easily be overcome with apprehension as this period approaches. However mystifying, a closer look reveals that it's a time that carries important hallmarks of growth and transition.

Navigating the tumult will take some parental savvy and an understanding of two important points. First, parents must recognize emerging behaviors and provide guidance to shape them. Second, they must accept that some of their children's previously mastered skills could be temporarily subverted while they are developing new ones. For example, a child who was taught to listen well might subvert listening to acquire better speaking skills. Or, teens may take new stands on when they will do homework or how they dress as they focus on negotiating driving privileges.

There is nothing wrong with these progressions. By embracing opportunities for growth, you can help kids prepare for life beyond childhood and avoid the landmines.

GENERATION GAP

As puzzling as they may be, teens display and amplify the most human of traits. On a daily basis they demonstrate the ability to seek novelty, create their own stories, and adapt to new environments. And it's all fueled by a turbo-charged brain that produces high-octane emotional responses combining to create a ferocious appetite for reward. Though hard to believe, it all really serves a purpose.

Thousands of years ago, with the very survival of our species at stake, it was not the forty- or fifty-something bankers, politicians, or lawyers who led us across the savanna away from the brink of extinction. It was the wily and willing teens and early twenty-somethings who led us to a more prosperous and less fatal future.

That teen brain chemistry, universal to all cultures to one degree or another, may well have survived natural selection to drive young adults to leave the safety of the home (or cave) to pursue the unknown. Teens' hunger for reward and novelty, and their remarkable ability to adapt and dismiss risk, was pure advantage for millennia.

On the flip side, a well-calibrated calculation for risk would have posed an obstacle. Our species would not have budged an inch without the whimsy and amplified drives of teens and young adults. It is clear that a more mature cognitive skill set that enabled reflection and risk assessment would have delayed or eliminated much of the progress of our ancestors.

For reasons that are still unclear, the time between the onset of puberty and full neurological maturity has grown due to early hormonal changes. What once may have lasted three years can now last as long as five or longer. This nebulous holding pattern, when the mind is still under construction, creates a gap for kids. Poorly managed and misunderstood, it can be a brutal time for all. The combination of unpredictable physiology and our modern existence requires psychological disc brakes to help pace the journey; otherwise, many kids in a blind rush toward adulthood will go right off the cliff.

The good news is that growth and learning can and still are happening. The difference is that we cannot hand our child ideas like cut flowers. We must plant seeds and provide him with soil so that they can grow from him. It is how his *independent self* can continue to grow.

These dynamic kids need help becoming autonomous, confident young adults. They need guidance to find their places as emerging citizens who create personal power by contributing to their futures rather than unknowingly putting their futures into jeopardy.

One thing is abundantly clear to anyone who has successfully engaged teens: when given the right opportunities, teens will work harder than any other group toward a worthwhile goal. And they have a track record to prove it. Here are some history-changing accomplishments that came at remarkably early ages:

- Thomas Edison's first sparks of invention flew when he was sixteen. Working as a telegraph operator, he devised an automatic instrument that did not require an attendant.
- Blaise Pascal was nineteen when he invented the mechanical adding machine.
- Louis Braille was fifteen when he developed the system of reading by raised dots.
- George Westinghouse, Jr. obtained his first patent for a rotary steam engine at nineteen.
- Mark Zuckerberg began his programming journey well before college; as a middle school student, he was working with the seed ideas of Facebook.

INERTIA: THE NEW DEPRESSION

Teens are not defective; they are emerging adults. However, the path to adulthood is not what it once was. As educational options, finances, marriage, sexuality, and job opportunities change before our eyes, pursuing dreams or making plans will not play out as they did in the recent past. Today's transition is much murkier than it was for past generations. Our snarky and fragmented world can make pursing dreams and surviving setbacks very difficult. A new strain of obstacle unique to the twenty-first century is surfacing. Inertia, the inability to change trajectory or put oneself in motion, is a real threat to the surge of energy that is necessary to propel adolescents forward.

Inertia and depression could be distant cousins. Both maladies put teens at risk for becoming aggressive or unruly. Achievement eludes kids who feel overwhelmed or are unable to garner resources or support to pursue their goals. As a last resort to effect change in their lives, teens without constructive forward motion can become destructive. They may resort to using shock and opposition to dominate a situation. Without accomplishment or vision for themselves, creating enemies becomes their only creative outlet or sense of control.

Just a breeze of personal injustice can remind these kids of their powerlessness and, in turn, trigger them to become disagreeable and lurch for power. With nothing to lose, these kids find that escalations can easily become a way of coping, a way of conveying, "I'm not afraid of you!" Their behavior is their way of shutting down the adult benchmarks and expectations that terrify them. Misguided choices, such as running up credit card debt, substance abuse, dropping out of school, or dysfunctional relationships, can be costly for kids. These kids not only miss opportunities, but they are undermining their futures. Ironically, they can appear so confident in their defiance of our directives that we forget that loss doesn't register for the under-twenty-one crowd.

It is the adults who carry that burden. We fear loss of opportunity, and sometimes life and limb! With kids' futures and our sanity at stake, parents must make sure that their kids are well aware of where their real power lies and how to enhance it. The difference between helping and hindering this process can be a fine line. Too much protection and vigilance against the downside of life can block the upside. Allowing teens some latitude and demanding accountability are a good start.

Shifting kids' awareness to competing with others is not the goal. As any elite athlete will attest, success comes when athletes are less concerned with their opponents and more focused on their own skill and performance. Self-defeating behaviors that become obstacles to learning and growth are the enemies. Getting that equation straight makes all the difference in who moves forward in life and who becomes trapped by inertia. Wasting this adolescent developmental energy poses a major setback and one of the greatest missed opportunities for young people.

READY FOR TAKE-OFF

Despite our best efforts, every home at some point will feel oppressive to our teens. Without alternative outlets for growth and expression, dissent becomes their only demonstration of growing up. If they are additionally being marginalized or infantilized by society at large, that combination will drive them to be more radical in how they express their primal need to matter and have value.

What kids don't realize is that shutting down shuts out options and resources. Winning a turbulent teen's heart and mind will help her build an identity that engenders the respect that she so desperately wants and needs. The goal is to harness her developmental energy and shift her focus from you as the opposition so that she can open her eyes to the great world beyond. All the cognitive skill, language development, social appetite, and ability to persevere that were downloaded previously need to be channeled.

> **Without alternative outlets for growth and expression, dissent becomes their only demonstration of growing up.**

It is clear that an earlier onset of puberty and unclear boundaries for adulthood allow for a bigger vortex of teenage trouble. Sorting out which behaviors warrant worry or concern can be challenging. Some clear markers can help parents become better positioned to respond in a productive way.

Drill down to the core of what matters: good judgment and accountability. They are foundational traits in successful lives, whether in picking a partner, managing a credit score, pursuing a profession, or keeping personal boundaries. All kids deserve life experience to help get them there.

What follows will shed some light on how to help our teens launch and land on their feet rather than crash before they can get out the front door.

ENTREPRENEURS OF IDENTITY

"I don't know my kid anymore!" This has been declared on many occasions by parents seeking help with navigating the teenage years. They are caught unaware by their child's morphing energy as they realize that past performance of their parenting script is no guarantee of future results.

We see this in moments when a kiss from Mom is no longer just a kiss but a potential source of devastating embarrassment for your teenage son or daughter. However, these seemingly endless awkward responses to the social and emotional challenges of adolescence have a purpose. As your children's motivations change, so should the role you play in their lives. Figuring this out will take time.

Logic tells us that parents' history with their children should give parents the edge at this stage of the game. This is not always the case, and success with counseling teens gives a clue. Ironically, the main ingredient to successfully counseling a teen is not your history with him; it is your lack of it. Too much history is like trying to change the ingredients of a cake that is already baked!

Any counselor worth her salt will capitalize on that blank slate to let the child slowly reveal what has been hiding below the radar. Understanding the teen years as a transition rather than a problem is key. Kids are looking to shed their history of dependency. As a result, they are driven to experiences that make them feel capable without you. Pushing away from you means walking toward a more independent self. Your words have less weight because they have the echo of dependency.

Peer approval is a critical element for teens. The primal directive to find safety in the pack away from home is not negotiable; however, it is temporary. Declaring independence is all part of the process and experience they will need to prove their worth. Just telling them how valuable they are will not deliver the hands-on knowledge that will transform them into thinking adults.

Instead of treating kids of this age as inscrutable and hopeless, think of them as entrepreneurs of their own identities. Obviously a lot of what harms kids is self-inflicted, but it is more a consequence of bad timing than bad design. While they are under this firestorm of change, teens must be able to select influences, suppress their impulses, and at the same time send the message that everything is "cool." It's our job to help them seize the opportunities that enable them to adapt and expand their options. Over time, applying the skills and lessons brought forward from childhood and combining them with real-life experiences is what will separate the adults from the children.

ENTITLED OR SEDUCED?

We are all offended by what feels like a sense of entitlement from our youth. Whether it is the relentless focus on a self-centered pursuit, achievement, or a reluctance to work, we share a palpable disquiet about how dismissive they can be toward effort. This can be even more pronounced when it comes to the menial or more humbling tasks in life.

Many have no clue as to what real-world effort even looks like, let alone feels like. *Seduction* is the real crime against their futures. Driven biologically by an increasing unwillingness to accept an agenda conceived by a parent, teens are left vulnerable to misleading messages from our culture. Daily, they drink from a well that obscures much of how the world works. Many of them really believe that success, wealth, fame, and fortune are just one casting call away. Very aware of ATM withdrawals, many never witness the toil that creates the deposits. Readily accessible fantasy can derail the hard-won focus and rigor that satisfying accomplishment really requires. In the absence of an alternative experience, they may not know about the substantive part of working through a challenge or toward a goal.

SPLIT SCREEN

Adult benchmarks, college entrance exams, saving money, or getting a job matter little to teens. They are far more inclined to be focused on their immediate world than a parent's future projections. At the same time, on a deep level, most are well aware that there is an adult world that they are ill equipped to navigate.

The problem is that their developmental energy will allow them to execute without a clear vision for themselves. Things can become obscured in a rush of unintended consequences.

It's different for adults. They can draw on personal experiences and conjure up a "split-screen effect" if they choose. Using their cognitive capabilities to imagine the impact of their actions or inactions, their goals or projected identity, adjustments can be made to keep life on track.

Mired in their adolescent bubble, teens can go through what feels like an identity crisis. Clumsy at establishing personal prerogatives, getting a clear vision of their internal split screen can be more challenging, but not impossible.

Recent research that explores the developing adolescent brain indicates that under the right conditions, kids can strategize and reason as well as any adult. A sense of self-determination, minus distractions, can push teens to use their brains in different ways.

A parent's energy is best invested in creating conditions that get kids to use their imaginations. It is how they will build connections to their larger future experiences. That means staying in touch with their immediate circumstances but consistently weaving their attention toward bigger rewards.

How adults guide teens to view experiences that offer immediate short-term rewards (shopping, iPhones, sleepovers) will determine many of the patterns that influence their future choices. The crucial inflection point happens when teens learn to imagine the next iteration on a mental split screen that links their effort of today to a future goal. Some call it doing the work of the crisis before the crisis happens.

A nineteen-year-old sat in a college classroom under a cloud of failing grades with not a signpost in sight to tell him where to go or what to do. On his own for the first time, piloting his own life, Mark had no vision for himself. During his first semester, he quickly lost his horizon. In the absence of the structure and propulsion that the journey from K–12 previously provided, parties and free-falling grades had begun to accelerate the spiral he had created for himself. Up until this point, Mark was fueled by short-term efforts and guided by the trappings of his K–12 education. Getting a good grade to appease his parents or sidestepping challenges that did not seem immediately gratifying directed his existence and energy. His parents often felt he was "lazy" and could accomplish so much more if he would just put forth the effort. They sent him off to college assuming he would find his way and decide to work harder.

They were wrong. He did not find his way. He found himself sitting in my office, begging me not to tell his parents that he was failing three of five courses and would probably be asked to leave school. Ashamed and confused, he knew he had let them down and wasted their money. In turn, he was avoiding them. He agreed to meet with me in exchange for use of their car over winter break.

We met several times. As we chatted, he revealed more and more about how he was jealous of people who knew not only what they wanted, but how to go after it. He was painfully aware that he had no traction or real direction in his life. He had doting parents willing to fix things and find resources for him. Unfortunately, their efforts were obstacles, as they blocked him from finding his own way. Mark was unable to connect the dots of his immediate actions with a larger vision for himself.

In today's less-structured world, it is imperative to provide your own structure. In many instances, the vision in your head will be the only guide you have! Mark had never held a vision for himself; his parents did it for him. Like many young people, he wasn't sure who he wanted to be, so he ended up doing nothing. Many of us assume that just because a kid gets good grades and stays out of trouble, she will navigate without the guiding light of home and hearth. Some kids must be taught that the freedom to be whatever they want requires a skill set. Kids need to develop the split screen in their minds. One side holds the circumstances they currently face, while the other holds a compelling vision for the future. Without that reference, daily efforts can lose their meaning, and the emerging adult can easily lose her way.

Understanding the connection between actions of the day and the future vision can be tough for an inexperienced mind. Two elements must be cultivated:

1. There needs to be an organic vision from the young adult. No matter how sparse or sketchy, it must make the young adult feel as if he is expanding himself and not being told what to do.
2. The ability to toggle between present challenge and future gain needs to be developed. An adolescent must not only be able to hold the two in stereo but be cognizant that doing so is necessary.

Mark did have a wisp of vision for himself as a veterinarian, but whenever he briefly mentioned it, his parents "shot him down," saying he would never finish the eight years of school necessary. As he sat in his History of the World, Digital Marketing 101, and philosophy classes, all he saw was a blank screen when he tried to figure out what the effort was all about, so he just stopped trying.

In many cases, it is the expectations of parents or the projections of society that direct a child's actions. Eventually it comes to a point that the child must conjure up a vision that provides fuel and direction for his pursuits.

REASONS ARE NOT REASONING

Invariably all kids will get in over their heads at some point. They become full of notions about rights but are delayed in considering responsibilities. That is when they discover that old rules don't apply anymore. The reality that their parents can no longer unconditionally label them as good kids in the face of bad choices can be quite sobering. Unable to self-reflect and identify problems, they dig the hole deeper. Feeling diminished, they lunge for power and create immediate costs not only for themselves but their families. Unfortunately, opportunities for teens to feel respected or valued by the adult population on the merits of who they are, are few and far between. It often plays out in scenarios like this:

"Why can't I just say no? I'm the parent after all!" Jenna's mother was frustrated with her sixteen-year-old daughter's increasingly demanding attitude. The relationship with her boyfriend was progressing too fast for her parents' liking. Requests for privileges were becoming demands. During their consult, they stated their concern that her thinking had become very black and white. Concerned that their once trustworthy daughter had begun to lie and showed no ability to meet in the middle, they became more punitive with her. Those measures only served to make matters escalate out of control.

Jenna's complaint was that she was treated like a baby. She felt forced to see me because she had been busted for staying at her girlfriend's house while her parents were away. The high school senior had been looking forward to all the freedoms her driving privileges and past good behaviors would bring, and now her plans had been short-circuited. Grounded and demoralized, she was at a complete loss of what to do.

Contrary to what her parents thought, Jenna had not lost her moral compass; she was just lost. Unable to resonate with her parents' reasons, rules, and expectations, she let her amplified appetite for rewards lead the way. And the problem was compounded by what was missing: the ability to reason for herself was glaringly absent from the equation.

In our sessions, together we reasoned through how to rectify the situation. First we identified her biggest complaint about being treated like a baby. Then we explored whether her behaviors warranted being treated like a young adult. Because she was unable to connect the pieces of her story by herself, we analyzed the details together. Little things like name-calling during a disagreement, failing to apologize to siblings, refusing to pay for her own gas in the car, and allowing her boyfriend to "grunt" instead of greeting her parents properly, all provided data points for her to reason through and connect. Ultimately she realized that she was directly contributing to her problem.

Newly equipped with the ability to reflect on her behaviors, Jenna was able to bolster her reasoning processes. The blame she placed on her parents faded fast when her own ability to reason began to steer the ship. She learned that until she provided evidence to others that she was a mature young adult, she would most likely continue to be treated like a child, not only in her home but outside as well.

SHOW THEM THE MONEY

Guarantee of financial success in the early stages of young adulthood is rare. However, early on, the specter of financial failure can easily take hold and put a drag on a young person's launch into life. In a world that thrives on the marketplace and immensely complicated financial instruments and transactions, it has never been more important to equip your child with hands-on financial skills and knowledge.

Too often young people have lifestyle expectations but don't have the financial knowledge necessary to achieve them. Blissfully unaware of the consequences, teens may think a luxury lifestyle is easily in reach with the swipe of a credit card. They are missing the real-world lessons that teach them how to build a foundation that leads to financial security. In the wake of crushing personal financial debacles, more than ever our next generation must have hands-on money management experience. Moving kids beyond knowing about money in theory is one of the most important legacies you will leave for them. Few people in their lives are better positioned than parents to help teens get on the right track to manage finances responsibly. There is no substitute for the judgment and accountability that can be gained from direct experience with managing and saving money. Studies show that instruction about finance without direct experience can put a young adult at higher risk for missteps than kids who have no financial knowledge. In other words, lectures about saving and other money management tips should come complete with deposit slips and a ride to the bank.

HORTON HEARS A WHO

It has been a widely held belief that shared perspectives positively influence attempts at empathy and cooperation. After all, shared context is the definitive glue of working relationships.

As with most things in life, timing is everything. Recent studies show that when a power differential exists between two parties and is amplified, the odds for cooperation are a little less reliable. This is especially true if things are already a little heated.

Researchers have found that if the less powerful party is made aware of the other party's power over them, there is a reduced chance of seeing eye-to-eye. Things can actually end up looking like an eye for an eye! This can be especially true for a teen mired in vulnerability.

Adults often make the mistake of amplifying a teen's powerlessness right when they should be minimizing those feelings and showing her the way to her power. Parents need to take the time to teach their kids how to communicate and really be heard. It is a time to hit the pause button on giving your perspective and let them give you theirs. They are trying to figure out who they are, and they don't want someone else to do it first.

Listening as a way of relating is key. Teens will need to feel related to before they can even consider relating to the needs of others. Listening to your teen does not mean you agree; it means he has value. We are so busy trying to stuff our children with information that they have little or no opportunity to practice finding their own voices.

Allowing conversations to deteriorate into a win-or-lose proposition is counterproductive. Your son or daughter will not stay engaged to lose. This also means that he or she will not have interest in what you have to say. Turning down our volume allows us to hear our kids' fledging voices through the noise of adolescence.

MENTORING

Research shows that teens and young adults don't so much lose their way as choose the wrong influences. With little experience or understanding of consequence, they can spin their wheels in futile directions for years. The loss of precious time and developmental energy can easily erode their once robust appetites for independence. An ounce of prevention is worth a pound of cure for this problem. The answer can be found in the power of mentorship, a crucial ingredient for our next generation that cannot be overstated. Ironically, parents are not always the best-positioned players in the lives of their children. Sometimes it is just wise to let other adults do the heavy lifting. They can give parental-grade guidance when tolerance for direct parental input is on the decline.

Keep in mind that over-reliance on Mom and Dad is an evolutionary harbinger of failure. Kids are wired at some point to block direction solely from the home front. This is an indicator of growth and a healthy reach to lead their own lives.

Encouragement and guidance from other caring adults is more important than ever. Not to be confused with caretakers, mentors are messengers. They are capable trail guides who point things out but do not do the walking for you. Whether they identify the deadline for a college application or that being late for work is a deal breaker, the key is to shine the light and walk away. Then, the teen can claim that space as her own and determine the agenda while gaining the sense of confidence and competence she so desperately craves.

Aunts, uncles, coaches, and neighbors are all good candidates to step up when parents need to step aside and let someone else lead the way from time to time. Achievements outside the influence of Mom and Dad can do much more than deliver pride—they can help inspire.

OPPORTUNITY KNOCKS

It's understandable that each generation wishes to make the next generation's life easier. Parents want to give ease, but in order for children to carve their own sense of identity, they need the opportunity to experience effort.

A sense of competence is a powerful motivator that validates people of all ages. Add a dash of respect, and that combination can be a potent elixir for what ails many of our teens. Desperate for confident identities, they can become vulnerable to the gravitational pull of social rewards. It is easy to belong to peer groups that provide membership but little sense of accountability. The experience ends up being as hollow as it sounds.

Lack of opportunity to garner real-life experience creates a tinderbox for the young and the restless. At this point, Mom, Dad, and the home front often end up in their crosshairs. Unfortunately, their sense of time, place, and opponent often needs recalibrating.

Finding the way to carve identities beyond those of their childhood can feel like defying gravity to many teens. Often they know what needs to happen. Organizing themselves, making priorities, and being and feeling dependable in the outside world are all intuitive capacities that they know they need in order to flourish.

Ironically, these kids are capable of identifying which of their friends and acquaintances are destined for success and which may crash midflight. They are keen to notice the habits of their peers that have value and those that don't. However, being able to spot a problem does not translate into being able to fix their own.

A well-timed conversation with a teen can provide some unguarded insight. Be careful to craft your message to convey opportunity rather than criticism.

Criticism: "Do you think I'm made of money? Quit being lazy and get a job if you want to buy that."

Opportunity: "Now that you are (whatever age), you may have an opportunity to make and save some money so you can afford that. Would you like to call a few stores in town to see if there are any job openings?"

Help children identify real-world opportunities where they can engage and develop a sense of accountability.

It is imperative that kids gain access to experiences that broaden their reach beyond social acceptance or academic achievements. Our kids need practical and personal economic participation and the growth that comes with it. That means getting a job, creating something of value, or committing to volunteer. All are acceptable avenues to cultivate a sense of autonomy and self-reliance.

The teen years are the perfect time to experiment, when stakes are low but the return on experience can be high. Exposure to the real world will foster skill in responding to uncertain or unexpected circumstances. Over time, trial and error on their own terms will teach teens that there is no real secret to success. They will learn the truth that consistently showing up and being accountable for outcomes will get them where they want to go.

The teen years are the perfect time to experiment, when stakes are low but the return on experience can be high.

PROMETHEAN REACH

Forging ahead and changing our world will require boldly creative and defiantly original young people. With proper guidance, they will not only converge with the adult world, but they will add value. The seeds of civil rights and equal rights for women were all born of this energy. Pace and patience will be required in their Promethean reach to emerge from clay figures in the minds of their parents. They will eventually become animated adults themselves with their own fires. Providing guidance to help them calibrate their internal compasses and navigate personal challenges can lead to big payoffs in their lives as well as your own.

CHAPTER 9

When a Bad Kid is a Good Thing

Discipline and punishment are separate but not equal.

ALL CHILDREN AT SOME POINT are compelled to act independently of the nurturing care of their parents. It is their way of obtaining some sense of control over their environments. These initial efforts toward securing a sense of power are far from perfect and often inefficient. In the absence of a good, viable alternative, otherwise well-behaved "good" kids will at one time or another act "badly." Understanding that these outbursts signal teachable moments can make a huge difference in what behavior follows. Too often kids will make poor choices, not as a result of something bad but rather in the absence of something good.

It is easy to overlook or forget that friction is almost always the precursor to growth and learning. Think about the elements in your life that have been outgrown. Outgrowing your home or car while expanding the family will always be punctuated by discord between family and space before an upgrade is made. Ever lose at a game before you learned to win? We all fall before we learn to walk. You would never punish a baby for struggling to coordinate his limbs in an attempt to attain points beyond his reach. The paths to mastering behaviors will have similar trajectories.

BEHAVIORAL SONAR

> To my own horror, I was chasing my toddler while she screamed "No!" repeatedly in response to my instruction to put her pajamas on. "But Mommy, if I take off my outfit, I won't be a fairy princess anymore!" Guess who slept in her princess outfit that night? Her *no* wasn't defiance; it was her only way to preserve her role as a princess.

Throughout their development, kids are busy taking in experiences and drawing conclusions about how to operate in the world. It takes a keen eye to know what may be going on beneath the surface for a child. Many of us can be quick to judge their not-ready-for-prime-time behaviors as character defects. Mostly driven by impulse and an increasing need for power, children's behaviors are often reactive and uncoordinated.

In reality, what is going on behaviorally is not always a true reflection of what the child is trying to communicate. Children act out when they do not have the skill to meet their needs or solve the problem at hand. This disconnect creates a deeply misunderstood vulnerability for kids, especially the young ones. Developing "behavioral sonar," the ability to determine what is driving the behavior below the surface, is key in achieving better outcomes.

Unfortunately, kids are often demonized for their bad behavior. Time and again moms and dads will be alert only to what they see on the surface. With that mindset, battles ensue, tantrums are triggered, and we hope to live to fight another day, usually about the same things. Too often, we assume that something constructive has happened during these skirmishes. That is rarely if ever the case. That "bad" behavior is actually a good thing, a locator of where your child is on her map of development. Shifting from alert to aware can usher in a whole new world of opportunities for parents and children.

In my household, chaos always ensued when my then four-year-old son would ban his sister from leaving the house by declaring, "You can't go outside!" She would push back with a "No!" and the battle would begin. As my son became a more social creature, his need for a playmate was lost in translation. Radar said: my son was looking to boss his sister around. Sonar translation: "I want you to stay inside and play with me because I like you!" He wasn't trying to push her around. As a four-year-old, he was doing the best he could to convey his wish for her to play inside. Reading the sonar of the situation, I knew that this child, appearing to boss his sister around, really wanted nothing more than to have a playmate indoors.

An exchange like that can be a good thing for an aware parent. It signals that my son needed help with his language skills. The exchange was a technical problem, not a belief problem. He did not really believe his sister couldn't go outside. He was using inaccurate language. As a result, the wrong message was sent. Will repackaging the request ensure compliance? No. But the response will be based on the true merits of the request and not a reaction to a technicality!

Take a moment to rethink situations that often culminate in standard, one-size-fits-all responses. We need to upgrade time-outs to parental "time-ins." When kids misbehave or break the rules, take a moment for a closer look. Remember, behavior is a barometer for children's developmental odyssey. In many cases, it will provide a neon sign that signals a need for help or guidance regarding what a child needs to learn.

Social dynamics in particular can shift very quickly for kids. We all have experienced the child who disrupts playtime for seemingly no apparent reason. Interfering with a game and ostracizing another child in the group are behaviors that seem to come out of nowhere. Unfortunately, many kids are at a loss about which behaviors will earn them acceptance. Left with a desire to belong, yet at a loss of how to interact, bad choices become part of the process.

Making the investment early on to identify what is going on for kids below the surface is vital. How we respond to children when they misbehave or make wrong choices is never just about the particular moment. It is about the larger context of making sure kids have an understanding of how to respond to everyday experiences. Parental intervention should focus on helping them keep options open and facilitating their ability to communicate and articulate their real needs and wants.

COLLATERAL DAMAGE OF PUNISHMENT

Punishing children as a means to control behavior has been a staple in our society for eons. However, using punishment to broaden your child's skill set is not the answer. It would be like trying to build a car from a bicycle. There aren't any parts available from the bike to build a self-sustaining motor for the car. Ultimately, one remains stuck.

Using punishment to elicit better results from a child presents a similar dilemma and causes collateral damage. It creates a dangerous feedback loop that is hard to measure. Being sent a message to be fearful of a parent or caregiver ruptures the connection between parent and child. The resulting anxiety can create a potent emotional challenge for kids trying to navigate twenty-first century stressors.

At the same time, it is impossible to overemphasize the boomerang effect of how we interact with our children, particularly during highly charged moments. Simple gestures such as overuse of the word "no," escalating in tone, or being physical to make a point can have impact beyond our immediate intent. They will prime kids to use those same strategies with us in the future. Consider this scenario:

> In the middle of a squabble about homework and chores, Chris, age eleven, grabbed a knife and leapt up on the counter, telling his mother to " leave him alone." She told him he

was scaring her. To her horror, he replied, "I know. This is what Dad does to me when he wants something."

Punishment may be an efficient method to control behaviors in many cases, but unfortunately, controlling behavior through punitive measures does nothing to help a child grow. It signifies a parent's lack of alternate resources and has no connection to how day-to-day life really works. In the heat of those moments, a child will rarely see you as a source of comfort or wisdom. His bias will steer him to see you more as threat than teacher.

Punishment keeps a child on alert for danger and ready to defend. In many cases, it just compels a child to be craftier at hiding his behavior. Avoiding you becomes an imperative. He soon learns that good behavior isn't the only way to avoid punitive measures; there are many options, including becoming adept at lying and manipulating. Skill in blaming or dominating others to reduce the threat can become central themes in how your child responds to authority. He begins to believe that if he can escape reprimand, his actions must be okay.

With some kids, harsh punitive measures are like weeding the garden with a nuclear bomb. Yes, you have killed the weeds, but you also killed the growth of other vital traits as well. Punitive measures could easily cause a more sensitive, reluctant child to shrink back from engaging with the world. People pleasing, poor self-image, and perfectionist tendencies can all be born of harsh upbringings.

At the other end of the spectrum will be those who identify with the aggressors in their lives. Kids can become punitive with others in an attempt to not feel so powerless. The crusty exterior they develop to protect against the fear-based punitive measures of a parent will become a part of who they are and how they acquire power in their world (see chapter 14, "Beyond Bullying").

If the presence of a threat is the only thing that stands between a child doing the appropriate thing and behaving badly, it is not such a stretch to think that kids will behave in outrageous ways when left to their own devices. School buses, backyards, and basements become breeding grounds for what they can get away with!

Dependency on threat and fear is a stopgap formula that will not prepare kids for the complexity of their futures. Every organism on the planet has an innate ability to adapt to unfavorable circumstances. Kids are no different. Children will adapt by preempting a threat with their own form of aggression to ensure self-preservation. The problem arises when that threat comes in the form of a parent.

Children learn from you how to respond in a threatening moment. Mother Nature designed it that way to ensure the survival of offspring. When our ancestors lived on the savanna, questioning a parent's actions could mean life or death. The signal to run is the signal to run ... no questions allowed. Limited cognitive function at young ages makes the absorption factor that much more efficient.

In many child-rearing situations, a parent's harsh words and a willingness to strike are all that are needed to download aggressive tendencies into a child. It is only a question of when for kids who feel preyed upon before they feel entitled to turn the tables on others.

Imagine how ineffective, or even impossible, your interventions will be when the child is echoing back what she learned from you at some later point in time. Remember, punishment often leads to the humiliation and shame that block growth in a young mind. While rupturing the connection between parent and child, it also diminishes a child's trust in others before her relationship with the outside world even begins.

RESOURCE OR ENEMY

Parents have been and will remain the most significant influence throughout a child's formative years. Biologically and psychologically, the cords that exist between parent and child have enormous impact on how a child learns to respond to the world.

Your relationship with your child has a dual nature: it determines his immediate experience, and at the same time determines his future outcomes. We not only need to be resources in the moment, but we also need to provide a resource for the future, a person he can return to as the challenges change and the world spins faster.

If your children are lucky, they will have many resources in their lives beyond Mom and Dad, people on whom they can rely to guide them when the stakes in life get higher. Unfortunately for many, postmodern life will not readily provide those resources. Fragmented families, the isolation of suburban living, and a faster pace of life have made those connections difficult. For these reasons and many more, the family, particularly parents, has a renewed importance. In many cases, parents may be the only resources they can count on.

Grown-ups somehow convince themselves that when the time comes for the serious stuff, what happened in the past will stay in the past for your child. It does not. Being animals of anticipation, humans rely on past events to determine future choices; it is how we avoid touching the hot stove or going back to a bad restaurant. Many of us expect that we can behave in clumsy, thoughtless ways, and our kids will filter this out, projecting an agreeable parental figure into their minds when they need it. This is rarely if ever the case. Fear and memory are partners. As a duo, they ensure that what or who a child is afraid of is seared into her memory.

A common thread for most kids "at risk" is their refusal to connect with their parents in a meaningful way. In an effort to avoid harsh punishment or be subjected to a parental "freak out," kids will choose to live closer to the edge of disaster rather than risk feeling the shame that punishment can deliver.

How we respond to children in their formative years will have an enduring effect on how they perceive us in later years. There will come a time when your child has choices beyond your reach. Poor modeling will not only neglect learning opportunities, but also compromise how your children perceive you as their world becomes more complicated.

Consistently defaulting to intimidation marginalizes children's ability to learn from their mistakes. It erodes their sense of self-reliance and perception of adults as resources. Moms and dads who routinely use shame-based methods to control behavior will find themselves in enemy territory with little latitude to make changes, especially during the teen years when it counts most.

Think of your early experiences with your child as an audition. Each interaction is leaving a legacy of who he can expect you to be in the future. We conserve our mental energy by relying on a CliffsNotes™, or condensed version of the people around us. We do not have to read a résumé every time we meet; our personal history with each other does the trick! Kids are no different when it comes to their parents. There will not be time or energy to reintroduce yourself in the years ahead. It's like a rock band going on a reunion tour. If people liked the band's old stuff, they will buy tickets for the show. If not, they will take a pass. However, it will be nearly impossible for the band to use that opportunity to introduce totally new material. Parents can face a similar challenge. Behaving like the enemy during the early years will not get you a repeat performance as your child matures.

The majority of families have well-laid plans for the good times. Vacations, birthdays, achievements, and holidays all carry a prearranged blueprint or plan for departure, destination, and arrival. Rarely do we have a plan for when things go badly. This void is where parents can face the most pitfalls and default to being the enemy. In the absence of a plan and tools to execute, we rush in based on our immediate feelings. Actions become driven by a muddle of impulses to remedy our own insecurities, control behavior, and secure love all at the same time. There's no chance for success in that mess.

Avoiding enemy territory with your kids requires better communication at earlier stages. A smart first step is to upgrade your approach to embrace sound discipline without the unintended consequences of punishment.

THE POWER OF DISCIPLINE

Humans gravitate to the familiar. We often have beliefs or behaviors not because they add value, but because they are what we are familiar with. What we make kids familiar with is what they will learn.

Mother Nature's plan provides that offspring are always preparing for some future date when parents will not be available to warn or protect. Kids will learn what we teach them. Even in the face of this well-worn path of learning, it must be remembered that friction-filled moments are most likely the precursors to learning and growth. It is in those moments that our kids will learn patterns that will drive their lives. How to respond and what to believe in the midst of that friction will either give them power, or take it away. Harnessing that power is a critical step in seeing a bad kid as a good thing!

Kids will learn what we teach them.

During development, it is vital for children to acquire habits of self-governance that provide them with a way to conduct themselves to attract what they want or need and insulate them from the bad and unnecessary. This will require power that conveys influence, not domination. How we respond to kids and their behavior will determine which form of power they will develop an appetite for in the coming years.

Punishment and discipline are often used interchangeably as if they describe the same thing. They do not. The differences between discipline and punishment are real and worth distinguishing.

Punishment is a method. It serves to foster detrimental imbalances of power between parent and child. Punitive measures require a victim and trade on fear. In most cases, parents do not want or seek to punish. Punishment often serves as a default when there is no plan. It is more like a day trade than investing in your child. Punitive measures are actions based on the immediate without consideration for the conditions that may exist in the future.

Discipline, on the other hand, is an outcome. What a child believes is how she behaves. Discipline is about building a belief system that will serve beyond the immediate. Kids today must navigate in the face of cultural noise that can be deafening to their internal voice at times. Formative years need to be dedicated to establishing an internal constitution that can guide and serve the child in various areas of her life. Experiences in education, finances, professions, relationships, and community participation will all be derived from what she believes and how powerful she feels.

Choosing to discipline requires an understanding of design. Bad design creates dead ends. Good design creates possibility. John Maeda, a leading authority on design, says, "A designer is someone who constructs while he thinks, someone for whom planning and thinking go together." This is a necessary ingredient for anyone handling children and helping them to learn how to respond in the moment and the future.

Along with awareness, good design, planning, and thinking are at the core of discipline in parenting. Responding to our kids with a plan that moves toward well-thought-out goals is good *parenting design*.

FAMILY EVENING AT THE IMPROV

Giving children the power to self-govern through a well-designed belief system does not have to come at the expense of adult authority, but it will come at the expense of our egos. Taking the reactions of children personally is the number one mistake most parents make, when in reality, kids just don't have practice with the behaviors that you want to see from them. Improvisation could help parents a whole lot with this challenge.

A troupe of improv actors is fascinating to watch, as the actors seem to react to each other in a coordinated way despite random, unscripted directions. No two situations are alike, yet they reach a shared understanding of where they want the story line to go. Rather than power struggles, rules of engagement keep all players invested and involved to achieve a successful outcome. Their secret? Practice and process. They are expert at methods that allow for the flow of the story without dominating it. One story line does not play out at the expense of another. To ensure that the exchange stays on track, the members anticipate shift and know what to do to keep the dynamics moving forward, always avoiding dead ends. They have a core discipline of what to do and sometimes, more importantly, what not to do.

Parents could learn a lot from improvisation. Practicing a principled system of responses can help a family absorb stressors yet remain stable. Encoding interactions with a few simple rules can have enormous power. It is a well-known law of nature that larger scale behaviors are driven by duplication of smaller scale patterns, whether negative or positive. Daily overeating leads to a lifetime of weight challenges. Weekly overspending leads to a lifetime of debt. This is also true in the positive. Healthy portions on a daily basis and regular financial balancing create patterns that lead to positive outcomes. But just being exposed to or told about these patterns does not equal expertise in them; it is the engagement over time that will produce results.

TOOLS FOR A LEGACY OF CONNECTION

As much as it is important to love your children, it is equally important to have the tools to influence them in our chaotic world. Preparing our kids for their futures is the prime focus of parenting. Without a template and tools to ferry them across to young adulthood, they will remain stuck on the shores of childhood.

Crafting that template has plenty of challenge. It is a mystery why certain children are more cooperative than others, but that has not stopped scholars at the Yale Parenting Center and their colleagues from across the Atlantic at King's College of England from taking up the challenge of changing the odds for a "good kid" versus a "bad kid" in any situation. Among others, they are providing a growing body of research indicating that subtle changes on the part of parents can have enormous impact on how a child responds.

It can be so easy to lose your way when the chips are down and the stakes feel high. Navigating those critical moments with responses that have some structure and design can make all the difference. However, the ambitious goal of staying connected to meaningful outcomes during disagreeable moments will feel like an emotional stretch for many.

Rest assured, no parent will ever be perfect when responding to kids in a difficult situation. It has been well established that genetics plays a significant role in how a child responds to the world, but it is also becoming clear that parents can do better if we take the time to become aware of the opportunities for improvement.

Tools in any arena exist to extend the range of conditions under which we can have success. A deficit of tools in a child's repertoire will always be pronounced during difficult moments, but difficult moments do not have to be detrimental. Knowing how to apply tools that make the most of this will serve us well if we learn how to work with them.

Curbing impulses and less mature reactions in kids can create a formidable challenge for any parent. Just as we instill mastery of math facts and the alphabet, we must engage kids in ways that provide a good foundation between parent and child. Sowing those seeds for growth and keeping an eye on tomorrow will develop tools that prove to be of value not only inside the home but in the world at large.

NINE FOR THE ROAD

Responding to kids in disagreeable moments will always remain an imperfect endeavor. Busy setting expectations for our kids, we forget to set expectations for ourselves. In these nine guidelines, parents and caregivers will find core foundational tools that will prepare us to be skillful when things go awry. With practice, you will be able to call upon them at any time in or outside the home.

> **Busy setting expectations for our kids, we forget to set expectations for ourselves.**

1. Pace

The pace of any interaction has a huge impact on its outcome. Taking your time and resisting the rush will get you around the bend and on your way. Going faster puts you at risk of losing control and crashing. The pace of how we respond to bumps in the road with our kids follows the same principle and carries the same risk for a crash. People who accelerate transactions miss opportunities to teach and redirect. It all becomes a blur, like a ride on an express train.

Slow down your responses. Give yourself a chance to be deliberate and maintain control of your words and gestures. In turn, you will be modeling for your kids how to be in control of theirs.

2. Clarity

Would you ever attend a sales call, negotiate the purchase of a car, or go into a business meeting without a clear idea of the purpose? Of course not. Even so, many of us barrel into situations with our children without enough clarity to keep us on message.

Parents in desperate need of time and energy cannot afford interventions that are at risk of becoming directionless and draining. We all have given our kids a gentle nudge to help with the dishes only to have it derail into a debate about past grievances or family fairness. Investing just a few seconds on the front end of interactions to stay clear and on message will result in kids responding more readily.

Clarity helps avoid traps that catch a parent digging in their heels to insist a child be flexible or yelling to quiet him. Retaining a clear goal in the face of push back from kids can help side-step all kinds of counter-productive behavior.

Parents who redirect with a clear purpose foster trust with their child. Even if the interaction goes off track, if a caregiver remains clear, that psychological structure allows for easier regrouping to get things back on track. Be clear, and eventually kids get the message!

3. Questions Are the Answer

Most professions of consequence have a checklist for safety and suc-cess. Surgeons, astronauts, pilots, and the like all give consideration to a list of questions before they begin their specialty.

Parents carry as much of a burden as anyone, yet we all chase an-swers instead of heeding our checklist of questions.

To update and retain influence with your kids, continually recali-brate your strategy with key questions that can become powerful tools for connection and direction. Here is a sampling of questions to ask yourself as you interact with your child:

- *Am I behaving as part of the problem or part of a solution?*
- *Have I taught my child the behavior I am asking for?*
- *Am I in charge of the moment or out of control?*
- *Would I accept my own behavior if the same behavior came from my child?*
- *Does this response have scalability? In other words, is it even feasible when my child grows six inches and gains sixty pounds?*

Think of your exchanges in their extreme form and in light of their future implications. Do they stand the test of time? If not, it is time to rethink your approach.

4. Show Stoppers

Too often parents are disappointed when they end up with the same challenges day in and day out. Efforts to direct young kids can easily become scattered and shortsighted and result in directionless exchanges.

We grow and learn by reward. Keeping a child's eyes on the prize is key. It will take setting priorities that are conveyed through a clear and consistent message about what must happen before the show goes on.

In his book *The Laws of Simplicity*, John Maeda refers to the difference between "need to know" and "nice to know." He points out how the curve of a particular challenge shrinks when it is categorized as necessary and not optional. Influencing a child's behavior can pivot on the same principle. Children need an environment that provides sufficient and compelling support for what it is you want to see. Whether the message is to pick up a bathroom towel or take out the trash, the expectation must be clear and leveraged. In other words, the rest of the child's world *stops* until the task is complete.

Lifelong patterns will emerge from the synergy of request and reward. Once children make connections, they will begin to map out their next actions in the direction of reward. "Show stoppers" in the home are a great way to begin the process because they provide incentive that supports kids giving up old behaviors in favor of new ones.

When it comes to show stoppers, less is more. Pick one or two behaviors that you would like to see modified, and attach them to an interest of the child. Any behavior that is well marketed, over time, will get a positive response.

Avoiding tasks that are time-critical is key. For example, doing the dishes or tending to a pet can't wait. Instead, go for things that are an easy holdout. Belongings must be hung up or tucked away before after-school activities begin. Friends cannot come over until the bed is made or clothes are off the floor.

Stick to the equation as closely as you can. Practicing accountability and self-reliance on this basic level will eventually hit critical mass and become a part of who children are and how they approach the world. Kids who build this type of foundation for their rewards are more likely to not only set goals but also ultimately reach them. Learning early on that their behaviors directly impact their world teaches them not only to comply but in some cases to *anticipate* requests.

5. Silence

The number one mistake parents make with their kids is "over-talking" them. By the teen years, kids will have developed a "talker ID"—whenever they hear your voice, they will block out the communication. Avoiding this may not be entirely possible; however, we can maneuver so that at the very least, the important stuff gets through.

Kids love to verbally joust with adults. It gives them a sense of control over the exchange. The only problem is that the jousting often drives the exchange to exhaustion with nothing but frustration to show for it! As important as it is to talk with our kids, it is equally important to create space for them to reflect. Extra words can give an excuse to deflect and create a distraction from behavior that needs to be reexamined.

Just as words can inflame a situation, silence can be one of the tools we use to tame it. The inaction and stillness of silence can be powerful tools. Not to be mistaken with the punishing kind, reflective silence can create very fertile space in our interactions and give children the chance to "listen" to themselves.

Instead of being baited into a verbal joust, consider silence. Once you have made your point or been on the receiving end of a runaway tirade, unplug and breathe. It will slow the pace of the interaction and give you time to design your next move.

6. Prototype

The key to capturing your child's attention is to provide a model for what you want to see ... and fast. Successful business leaders are well acquainted with providing timely models for customers to instill confidence in new ideas. We cannot promote big ideas without tangible prototypes or samples of how things should work. Kids need that same treatment.

Children spend hours, sometimes days, playing with prototype toys. They stir up trouble with play kitchens and rule the roads with toy cars. They use mock-ups of real life imitating what they see around them. Banging pots and pans or sitting in the car progress to cooking or driving as the concepts become more familiar. Eventually there is a jump to real life, thanks to their experiences with prototypes.

Improving a child's behavior will require a similar effort. Many of us unwittingly block progress by trying to get our kids to move forward with prototypes that won't make the jump to better behavior. Common default parenting behaviors, such as dominating or escalating situations, inconsistent consequences, or poor boundaries, are just a few of the default prototypes that get the most exposure. Some households even lack a basic prototype requirement for household chores!

Remember, children are not free to choose behaviors that they don't know or have not mastered to some degree. It is difficult for them to learn without a model or concept with which to work. Suggesting to a sixteen-year-old that laundry needs to be done will have a far better success rate if the child has been prototyping the chore for the past decade. Dads doing dishes or making meals is the ultimate proof of concept for an adolescent male on the verge of launching into young adulthood and self-reliance.

Every expectation, from cultivating a confident handshake to acquiring table manners, will have a much higher success rate if a model for the behavior is within reach. Kids need to live what you want them to learn!

7. Punt

We will all encounter those perfect storm moments when we will not have the time or space to direct things as we would prefer. Whether in public or in a time crunch, caregivers will often be forced to use what they have at hand and work the moment.

In football, a team punts to relinquish the ball on their terms while making it more difficult for the other team to score. Parents sometimes find themselves in a similar situation with their kids. The challenge is to keep it on your terms. That means adults sometimes have to look for creative ways to retain authority, regardless of how small the concession from the child may be.

In other words, faced with a downward spiral at Target or a meltdown at mealtime in a crowded restaurant, parents, on occasion, will need to create upside with a compromise for these "special" circumstances.

Keep in mind that kids don't want to be in total control of any situation. That is a terrifying proposition for any child. Parents can make minor adjustments that can help them maintain authority of the unfolding situation in a positive way. Insisting that their child take a deep breath or add "please" or use words rather than meltdown to express what they want are good examples of punting. These are small transaction costs that keep the child connected to your identity as an authority and not just an obstacle. At the same time, you are providing an exercise in self-control.

There will inevitably come a time when your child must ask for concessions from family and friends. Having seen her parents model this, she will have the confidence to do so and remain in control.

8. Cool Your Engine

Every household will have its share of heated moments. They are unavoidable.

Heat is a physical property that changes everything. There are many professionals, from Wall Street traders to car mechanics and surgeons, who must wait for inflamed situations to cool before they begin their work. They are well aware that tinkering during the heat of the moment is at best a waste of time; at worst, it can cause more damage.

Every mom and dad I know has, at one time or another, made the classic mistake of overreaching in the heat of the moment. Over-talking to make a point or escalating to gain dominance will only serve to alienate and discourage everybody concerned.

It has been well established in the archives of neuroscience that a person's mind gripped by fear or anger cannot take in or process new information. In essence, there is a block on messages for future use. A hot head diverts us to the threat of the moment and nowhere else.

Having a heated moment does not have to be a dead end. It is just a signal to wait. Children need to know how to summon the energy to resolve problems after the flood of anger has subsided.

Utilizing cooler heads eliminates the need for fight or flight. That is when parents can create teaching moments instead of just hoping for them.

9. Humility

If being a parent is the hardest job in the world, being a *good* parent is the most humbling! The challenge to embody who and what you want to see from your kids is by far the most difficult aspect of parenting. But it has to be done.

The unintended shame and humiliation that can accompany parental reactions to misbehavior can destroy the connection between parent and child. Unable to repair, children are left steeped in confusion and unresolved feelings.

Too often there is impact and fallout from a parent's missteps that are not immediately seen and then assumed not to exist. A display of humility by a parent can change all of that. Kids need to know how to interactively repair a broken connection with a loved one. Acknowledging faults or correcting missteps are critical ingredients to that reconnection.

If being a parent is the hardest job in the world, being a *good* parent is the most humbling!

Teaching kids the ability to show humility stands in a category of its own. A comfort level with accountability could be the most pivotal trait a child can master.

We cannot always be there physically to guide and prompt our children in a sometimes-unforgiving world. They will face encounters that will require a skill set for rising above situations, repositioning, and reconnecting. Our job is to provide them the tools and guidance to interact effectively under a wide range of circumstances. And by relying on core guiding principles, modeling good behaviors, and setting realistic expectations, we will be successful at helping children develop the attitudes and behaviors that will serve them throughout their lives.

CHAPTER 10

Academics of Play

ALL WORK AND NO PLAY once made Jack a dull boy. However, by to-morrow's standards, being dull will be the least of his worries, as play-deprived Jack may just find himself disenfranchised and unemployed.

Until recently, many of us considered childhood play a quaint relic from the past. For decades, there has been an ongoing debate about the utility and impact of candid and unobstructed activity, and whether it is even necessary. As a matter of fact, play not only is necessary; it's essential.

Mounting research on the subject has tipped the scales so greatly it may even put pen and paper learning for young minds to bed and make ringing the recess bell a top priority. It is clear that unfettered, undirected play may be the most cutting-edge opportunity you can give your child. Play is an essential vitamin in cultivating stress reduction, anxiety management, and resilience—the mental health trifecta for a developing mind.

Is it optional? Not a chance.

Think of unstructured playtime as "mental play dough." It *requires* and *inspires* effort from young minds. In the process, children build upon ideas and strengthen mental muscles. Language skills are challenged and expanded; social skills are given the room to evolve naturally as kids collaborate and organically grow their ideas together. And, significant neurological research reveals that when children engage their senses and motor capabilities, they are priming the pump for critical thought and higher-order thinking down the road. Working memory, social intelligence, and a sense of mastery are all given a turbo charge in the process.

Creating context in the imaginary realm of dinosaurs or Star Wars is the precursor to sharing innovative ways of thinking, living, and finding solutions—all essential capacities in modern adult life.

The truth is that allowing children to play freely is the one parental responsibility that requires the least amount of effort. All children are born with an enormous capacity for creative thinking; in fact, they crave it. Their intelligence innately chooses to roam the terrain, capturing multiple sights, sounds, and sensations all at once.

Take note next time you give your kids a little free time. In a flash, pots and pans become musical instruments. Stories and adventures emerge, twisting and turning on a single whim. They can even show high-stakes, reckless abandon by wearing Halloween costumes in July to the grocery store. Pretty entrepreneurial, wouldn't you say? Play not only emboldens kids to think outside the box, but it allows them to shatter the box with impunity—as long as they stay away from the lamps in the living room!

YOU CAN'T FLUNK OUT OF RECESS

Fear of "failing" is enemy number one to a child's intelligence. If this fear is not addressed at a young age, it can taint opportunities and lead to self-sabotaging and excessive self-consciousness. Viewed in this light, play is also prevention. It insulates a child's inventiveness, courage, and flexibility far from any failing grade. Ample opportunities for children to play freely may encourage some of the most vital activities that pave the way to future success.

From an evolutionary perspective, play has carried out an essential role in the survival of many creatures, including humans. It offers the opportunity to respond to unexpected, random events and rapidly changing storylines. It cultivates the ability to innovate and sustain a creative endeavor beyond immediate resources. In today's world, preparation to respond to the uncertain with a capacity to create and innovate gives a huge advantage over those unable to respond and adapt.

PARENTS ... LET THE GAMES BEGIN!

Don't be fooled by marketing claims of accelerated brain development if you purchase a certain toy. It's like sexy advertising—wishful thinking with no solid evidence of a guaranteed outcome. In reality, creative play is an inside job. It is a direct offshoot of curiosity and divergent thinking. Many of the gadgets available to children are more about external performance and pushing buttons rather than real learning. During play, they learn to harness their energy to make something happen through tapping into their natural creative forces. All the while, this natural process produces a sense of reward that can fuel interactive learning for a lifetime.

Here are a few ideas to get their creative juices flowing:

- Everyday objects can be powerful tools of innovation and learning. Anything that makes sound is music. Laundry baskets, containers, and pillows are engineering materials. Mud pies are chemistry experiments, and tossing a ball (outdoors of course) is a foray into physics.
- Encourage your kids to formulate storylines and act them out. Playing with ideas is the initial stage of creating reality.

The mental imaging required for imaginary play can be as strong as 3-D reality.

- Take time to notice if your child is gravitating toward a natural interest. Most innovations are a direct result of someone pursuing a natural interest or curiosity while keeping his day job. Love of an interest is the greatest motivation for learning.

Remember three words: *Free, fun,* and *unfettered.* Keep these three concepts top of mind, and you just can't fail!

CHAPTER 11

Education Is Not a Spectator Sport

DECADES AGO, PARENTS' INVOLVEMENT IN their children's studies was never a big factor for determining educational success or failure. Many of us remember a time when parents could remain on the sidelines, jumping in on a science fair or two, and leaving the formal education to the experts. Why not? The formula was simple back then: reading, writing, and arithmetic. Spanish? Yes. Chinese? Never.

The entire education system was in a straitjacket—planned, controlled, and measured by test scores. The sole purpose of an education was to make all our kids economically viable in the most routine way possible. Our system prepared our children to get jobs, American jobs. Ah, the good old days.

But the era when a rudimentary education scored a ticket to a living wage has come and gone. Being sentimental about it is not only a waste of time, it is dangerous—for the future of our kids, for our world, and frankly, for us.

Have you noticed? Our education system is collapsing under its own weight, like a big ship lost at sea, tossing beneath an overwhelmed crew as it hollers, "No child left behind! No child left behind!" Take a closer look, and you see there is no chance that anyone will be left behind—an ill-prepared, poorly educated, noncreative workforce is right here, creating a huge drag on us all. Current economic conditions are a major red flag, a signal telling us that there is a dire need for an upgrade of American capabilities. The traits of perseverance, communication, and innovation will trump the ability to memorize dates and ace the SATs in the very near future. Unlearning familiar material and making room for innovative thinking will be as important as teaching.

Let's face it: traditional students have gone the way of the rotary phone, and they are not coming back. Traditional teachers had better step up their games, or they will be voted off the island as well. In the coming decades, a strong ability to learn will be a hedge against being taught outdated material. The need has never been greater for educators who understand that the material at hand is inconsequential compared to the actual process of how it is learned. *Teaching* does not have scalability or a multiplier effect over a child's lifetime, but the *learning process* does.

Okay, so put away your disguise, and drop the car keys. No need to run and hide. Transitions like this will, and should, feel like a crisis. We all know by now that every crisis or wake-up call presents an opportunity. This one is virtually screaming for parents to become partners in education. Textbook manufacturers and teachers unions run a distant second behind the influence parents have in their children's educations. Without collectively deciding to be part of the solution, we are, in effect, becoming part of the problem.

I'm not talking about attending more school board meetings or creating more fundraisers. We need to focus not only on

Teaching does not have scalability or a multiplier effect over a child's lifetime, but the *learning process* does.

preparing schools for our children but on preparing our children *for their world.*

HOMEWORK ASSIGNMENT FOR MOM AND DAD

Be the "home team." Partner with your child's school. Make the material she learns at school significant in her daily life. The more relevance you can add to her learning experience, the greater influence the process of learning will have in her life.

Embrace failure! Sometimes it is the *only* route to learning. Consider that a child can perform well on a test and never learn a thing.

Remember that effort trumps smartness over the long haul. It is not a stretch to see how praise for being smart could backfire with kids. Children easily can become reluctant to stretch themselves when presented with tasks that jeopardize the euphoric feeling of being "smart." Praising *effort* is a main ingredient in motivating a child to learn. Connecting his level of effort to positive outcomes gives the child power. Access to this formula will serve him for the rest of his life.

The next time your child does well on test or activity, say "Great job." The next time she doesn't do well, say "Great opportunity." Approach the topic with enthusiasm and possibility. Show her how to embrace the challenging, the daunting, the stuff that just doesn't come so easy.

Lastly, have a vision of your child beyond the classroom. Problem-solving and negotiation skills paired with decision-making and cooperation capabilities will be indispensable traits for future success. All of those skills have real estate in your child's home life. That "classroom" belongs to the parents. It's time for you to get in the game and make the grade.

CHAPTER 12

Forget "The Talk" and Start "The Walk"

*Developing healthy sexuality will require more
than just a talk with your children.*

IT SEEMS CRAZY, BUT EXPLORING the "birds and the bees" with our children still has the power to unhinge even the most confident adult.

It is that other parent, Mother Nature, who pipes up and ruins our dance with denial. She slams us with the inconvenient facts of life, facts that say developing a sexual identity is as natural as losing baby teeth. But it is not the facts that stand in the way of healthy sexuality; rather, it is the gap between the natural and necessary expansion of sexual identity and the onset of sexual contact. The space between a dependent childhood and the emerging independence of adolescence is fertile ground for exploring the new and novel. What grows there depends on what seeds we sow.

Many of today's moms and dads weren't raised by parents well equipped to discuss or discover their own sexuality. Reducing it to taboo for fear of pregnancy or corruption of moral codes left little room for discussion. Today's world and influences make the topic inescapable. While that makes some parents cringe, the environment provides a golden opportunity to guide our children in a way that allows them to better understand themselves and their emerging tensions and appetites.

Our responsibility is to help our children prepare to navigate relationships that don't involve Mom and Dad. Pleading for abstinence or leaving kids ignorant as the only options can be very risky. Acknowledging that Mother Nature wired them for sex frees us up to do our job: show them that they are *worthy of relationships*. The talk is information about their bodies and sex. The walk contains relevant, compelling information about themselves, their emerging creative identities, and their relationships.

Owning the reality that our children are emerging, complex individuals who will eventually work, love, and play beyond our reach allows us to deliver what really matters: *information about themselves*.

Media influence is strong and pervasive. Creating *immunity to the message* is key.

MISTAKEN IDENTITIES

As teens look to open up their worlds beyond home and school hallways, they will allow whatever our culture delivers to fill the gaps. In the twenty-first century, the world delivers the message of sex.

As a result of being bombarded with that message through a multitude of media forms, teens are dealing with the force of their own sexuality earlier and earlier. Motivated by profit, marketers will use every tool in their arsenals to direct your child's developmental imperative to "grow up" in order to feed their bottom lines. We have come to accept the images of scantily clad teenage girls and shirtless boys on shopping bags and billboards as a harmless feature in our children's world. It's not. It fills a developmental gap with garbage.

Marketing messages can alter children's perception of themselves. The steady stream of sexually charged material that oozes into their lives easily detracts kids from developing other aspects, mushrooming at a time when they cannot afford to be sidetracked. Without a basic identity to defend, or without a strong identity beyond appealing to the opposite sex, an unmitigated sex drive blocks their ability to discover and explore other aspects of themselves. Adrift in a world heavily influenced by the gratification of others, the young mind becomes reduced to a barometer of "hot" or "not hot."

TIMING IS EVERYTHING

The fear should not be about teens giving birth to babies. The real fear is teens not giving birth to themselves.

Adolescents become sexual because they must. It is the driving force of evolution that breaks their bonds of dependency on their family of origin. The problem is that evolution did not account for secondary education, employment outside the tribe, or the STDs that have been a steady companion of modern life. Left unexamined and strongly influenced by environmental forces, sexual energy can make kids feel like card-carrying adults. Engage these kids, and you'll quickly find out that they interpret one's ability to titillate and appear sexual as an indicator of adulthood. The temptation can be especially potent when they are desperate to prove they are indeed no longer children. Intent on being taken seriously, their appetite for being grown up can easily betray them.

Without demonizing sex, adults need to address the timing as the enemy. It is prime time to cultivate teens' expectations of themselves and their relationships beyond sexual gratification.

SUGAR AND SPICE ISN'T ENOUGH

Without a proper understanding of emerging sexual energies, young girls are surprised, confused, and terrified about the reactions they elicit from being sexually objectified. In truth, they are eliciting reactions way beyond their skill sets.

Societal pressures of submission and obedience can make it feel impossible to develop a sense of self-preservation. Girls need an identity that allows for acceptance and connection on terms that work not only for the moment but the future as well.

Assuming that a girl will snap back to her plans after the shock to her system of being seen as a sexual object is not enough. Early language skills and strong environmental support for girl power can give girls' goals an early edge. However, it is well known in psychological circles that females fall harder and faster in this developmental space. Keeping stride in the face of challenging outside influences is key. As her sexuality emerges, offer guidance to help your daughter understand that it should complement her identity and be harnessed to navigate her dreams—not eliminate them.

BOYS WILL BE BOYS ... IF WE LET THEM

Most of the fretting that we do about kids and sex is skewed toward girls and what they are inviting into their lives. Damaged reputation, abuse, pregnancy, and disease easily come to mind as vexing problems for young ladies coming of age. Somehow we assume that boys either know all they need to know, or that we can speak to them on a "need to know" basis.

Both postures are wrong and unfair to our boys in their quest to become men. It's a quest that they know about but rarely articulate for fear of breaking what many call the *boy code of silence,* which not only deadens spirits but the opportunity for boys to grasp what it really means to become a man. It is a little-known fact that General Patton was a poet. It has long been forgotten that George Washington had a penchant for interior design and a love for puppies and ponies that rivaled what he felt for Martha and his fellow countrymen. Poetry and paint chips are hardly masculine pursuits, yet they are abundant among profoundly powerful men.

When boys are otherwise awkward and reluctant in many aspects of relationships, becoming sexual offers a shortcut to a sense of manhood. The immediate arousal and gratification can make the effort of building a real relationship seem like too much work.

How do we raise boys to express their sexuality without getting lost in an ocean of impulses? Everywhere a boy looks, being sexually active is associated with status and power. *Why should I not partake in the pleasure that is offered? Why should I impose limits?* Once out of the nest, the answers to these questions become evident very quickly.

At seventeen, Jake seemed to his friends to have it all. A good student, he was a star athlete, drove a great car, and bragged about his sexual conquests. But his rhetoric didn't reflect the despair that was brewing within. His mom expressed concern that his grades were starting to slip, he was spending money excessively, he was missing college application deadlines, and he had garnered several driving infractions. Jake reluctantly visited me, shrugging off his parents' concerns and declaring he was "fine."

What I discovered was a young man who had an appetite for adulthood but no perspective of what it meant to actually be an adult. Jake was unraveling. Seeing it as a sign of weakness, he avoided asking for help.

We worked together on harnessing his appetite for adulthood, and refocused that energy on creating real relationships that would expose him to a full spectrum of emotions, not just the impulsive bursts of emotion that had given him immediate satisfaction.

We explored the notion that the façade he constructed through his behavior actually made him feel powerless. Jake slowly discovered that asking for help and imposing self-limits were building blocks for strength, not signs of weakness. Ultimately, he was able to accept his parents' support and guidance and gain direction to navigate the journey to real adulthood.

Men will be separated from the boys as surely as a boxer will take down a street fighter. Once they "man up" to the fact that anybody can throw a punch, just like anyone can have sex, they realize that self-control gives them opportunities for growth. They are then able to develop the emotional intelligence necessary to impose limits and harness energy in ways that honor their dignity and that of others.

THE BEGINNING OF MEN, NOT THE END OF MEN

Prolonged fixation on sexual gratification actually limits masculinity. It has real potential to block out the things that will truly allow boys to become men.

Boys need to know that taking on challenges in life requires resilience. It requires power that is not dependent on the weakness of others. Knowing you have what it takes to manage thoughts and feelings in a range of situations is critical to everything, from controlling impulses to setting goals.

If stuck on the treadmill of lust, boys are inviting the exact experiences they are so desperately trying to avoid. Loneliness, disconnection, shame, dependence, and isolation are all unintended consequences of sexual gratification that also impede one's ability to be in a relationship.

Boys' journeys up until this point must make it abundantly clear that the precursor to controlling conditions and building a successful life is self-control.

Parents need to go for the bull's-eye by delivering a clear, consistent message that relationships don't have a finish line; instead, they are ever changing with stops, starts, feelings, fears, and frustrations. Those experiences are all part of the process of becoming a man who has a plan beyond high school hallways.

SMART FROM THE START

Is it possible to help kids be smart from the start? That means laying a foundation during early childhood to guide children to be well prepared to meet all kinds of complex problems that arise in relationships, and keeping them on track as they mature.

This walk with your child is the last great opportunity your have as a parent to influence your children. Most encounters after that point will be diluted by outside forces that encourage kids to engage each other sexually, whether they are ready or not.

Think in terms of providing children immunity from a virus. An immune system never goes off duty. It has the ability to neutralize invaders even if contact is made. Kids today come in contact with information that is like a psychological virus. Notions about sex masquerade as adult competencies and need to be blocked and countered. The influences are not new. It is the virulence of the strain that has mutated into a formidable threat to a young mind. Going after the source is a waste of time. Creating immunity to block these influences is the way to go. Anticipating the harm and preparing a response will not only serve a teenager in the moment; it will provide protection in the years ahead.

THEY WERE BORN THIS WAY

For starters, remember, it is not a question of "if" kids will be interested in being sexual; it is a question of "when." The process is coded in their DNA.

The changing environment of contemporary lifestyle and heightened outside influences have converged to produce a very uninhibited, sexually charged group of youngsters. If sexuality is misunderstood, it can derail them from their futures.

I say "misunderstood" because I believe there is a silver lining. Sexual energy and creative energy are derived from the *same place* in our psyche. Once this truth is acknowledged, an adolescent can begin to harness the energy in a way that *expands* his or her life, rather than *derails* it.

In his classic book, *Think and Grow*, Napoleon Hill says, "When driven by this desire, men develop keenness of imagination, courage, willpower, persistence and creative ability unknown to them at other times."

This is not a reflection on promiscuity. It is an observation of someone acutely aware of the parallels between creative impulses and emerging sexuality. Both are a call to expand oneself into the world. The problem arises when creativity is mistaken for a signal to engage in acts of sex. Many geniuses have been doomed by lust, leaving brilliance behind on the bedroom floor.

Similarly, many kids are derailed because they don't understand the difference between sexuality and sexual activity. Sexuality emerges from what we feel. It is an expression of a desire to expand ourselves, very similar to creative energy. Any person who has pursued a creative endeavor knows that creative energy begins in the body and expands outward. They also know that harnessing creative energy takes time, discipline, and a period of trial and error before the outcome is ready for prime time.

Many geniuses have been doomed by lust, leaving brilliance behind on the bedroom floor.

For many teens, being sexual is giving rise to the strongest feelings and desires they have ever had. It leads to their sense of self-concept as their perception of themselves outside of the family's influence begins to emerge. It is a desire to experience themselves in a sensual way that reveals who they are and what they want to attract into their worlds.

It is an all too familiar story. Kristin's mother had been alerted to her daughter's Facebook postings by a friend. Unbeknownst to her mother, Kristin had been sexually active with several boys in her school and was now in a great deal of emotional pain. Panicked, her mother lamented that her daughter had so many hopes and dreams that were now dashed. I met with Kristin shortly thereafter.

Known as an artist, Kristin was always a "pleaser," with sensitivities so exquisite that she was unable to even swat a fly. No one could figure out why she always said yes to sexual contact. In some instances, she did not even know his last name.

At the tender age of fourteen, she was naive about the intentions or emotional ignorance of many of her peers. Kristin's natural artistic appetite and desire to experience herself in a more sensual way was being hijacked by acts of sexual contact. At a time when her identity as a creative being should have been expanding, it was being distorted. Without a framework to understand what was happening, her hopes and dreams were being crushed too.

Kristin needed the tools to harness the changes she was experiencing and the language to process them in a way that would build her world, not destroy it.

By helping her realize that the positive feelings that emerged when she produced great art propelled her to fulfill her dreams, she was able to silence the outside pressures and listen to her inner voice. She developed the ability to redirect the creative energy that was pulsing through her to connect with something beyond her childhood. She was able to build a creative identity beyond sexual contact.

Kristin is now in control. No longer racked by shame and better able to reflect on her choices, she is comfortable saying no. No longer mistaken about her identity, today she looks forward to who she is becoming and remains clear about who she is not.

A parent's call to protect is really a call to provide children with a process that preserves their creative forces, one that acknowledges emerging desires within children that strengthens their identities so they become more than just sexual partners.

POST-CHILDHOOD PLANNING

Once a child's schedule begins to deviate from the family calendar, it is a reliable indicator that post-childhood has set in. Soccer skills and SAT scores are no match for the adult pleasures and pressures that reside in the brains and bodies of our adolescents during this time.

The ground covered in post-childhood is very fertile for the right ideas and direction to take hold. Parents who are able to think in the future but act in the now will help their kids maximize this time by encouraging them to build strong identities. The strength of that identity is the best defense against the other elements looking to take up residence.

FIRST-TO-MARKET ADVANTAGE

Too often, parents squander their ability to influence their kids because they don't realize how powerful their input really is. You have the advantage of being in control of their resources and the ability to download undiluted messages for at least a decade. It is important to use this advantage before you lose it to the music, peer groups, clothing brands, and countless other elements that are vying to influence your children's attitudes and beliefs. The competitor's message is telling them that being sexually active should be part of their lives now and that everyone their age is doing it.

To keep their edge, parents need to unleash their own marketing campaign. Savvy and sophisticated, the message and messenger need to be clear, consistent, and confident—not trying to win or to reject a child's sexuality but embracing sexuality as a natural part of a child's maturing identity.

SEXUALITY IS NOT THE ENEMY; THE EMPTY SPACE IS

Kids need to know that sexuality is a part of healthy development. They also need to know that you are not against it. Removing the forbidden fruit aspect gives some room for influence and dialogue. Kids need language to talk about an emerging sexuality so that it pertains to more than just sexual contact. Initiate conversations that address this unfolding energy as part of something much bigger. Explain that it is an energy that arises like any other passion; for instance, motherhood, artistic expression, competition, and the desire to travel all draw on passionate, creative self-expression. Provide context so that they recognize sexuality as yet another form of a creative, emerging self.

Your message should acknowledge that developing interest in sex is normal. It is a wonderful part of our *creative identities* that is completely different than the act of sex. Sexuality helps an adolescent attract elements, people, and experiences that reflect not only who he is but who he is becoming. Acting on sexual impulse in the absence of a bigger concept of self is where the ugly stuff starts. Sexual energy that is only processed through acts of physical gratification attracts perceptions and beliefs that are not only shortsighted but dangerous.

Imagine driving a car without a steering wheel. You will get somewhere, but not a place of your choosing. Encourage teens to be in the driver's seats of their lives and fill the space that childhood leaves behind with pursuits that make them feel not only like they are growing up but that they are growing in directions of their choosing.

MORALITY IS NOT THE ISSUE; MENTALITY IS

Focusing on morality at a time when adolescents are at the mercy of hormones and neurological mayhem wastes precious time. It will take more than a blast of shame to shout down the new voices in their heads. Besides, shame only makes a child feel bad about herself. Ironically, it can serve as a motivator to do something that will make her feel good … which in many cases will be to engage in sex!

Kids are better served if we focus on "above the waist" skills, the constructive mental habits and tools that will serve them over a lifetime.

Keep in mind that kids tend to run away from what they don't understand. Today's world makes it difficult to prepare them for a future that we barely understand. But even in the face of this challenge, we can share with them what we do know. We can dispel the myths that say that driving a car, spending money, and having sex add up to a successful adulthood.

Look for opportunities when your child mentions someone he admires. Make it clear that successful people have a certain "mentality," a personal system for processing the thoughts and information they get every day, that helps them delay gratification and assess their environment for "value-added" propositions.

Just engaging in sexual contact doesn't bring kids any closer to the freedoms of adulthood they so desperately crave. Teach them to recognize that the quality of thought and ability to think through internal choices has the power to create or kill their hopes and dreams. It is their ability to assess situations and make choices that translates into making, or more accurately designing, their world.

PORTABILITY IS KEY

Most of what our kids are up against won't present itself to us at the kitchen table, so the tools that will be most effective are the ones that can be considered portable; in other words, they need tools that can be used outside of your reach and on the street.

Questions Are the Answer

Questions are the most portable tools in the world. A perfectly placed query can be very powerful. In their pursuit of power, boys and girls need time to learn that controlling oneself is the first step in controlling one's environment. Adding time to any decision-making process increases the quality of the decision made. Downloading a script that incorporates questions and not just directives can be started in early childhood.

The most important knowledge a child or person can have is self-knowledge. Stopping to ask yourself a question provides the detachment necessary to assess. It is the guiding force behind success in how to move forward in any endeavor, sexual or otherwise. It is only achieved with the ability to question yourself and honestly examine your answers.

A parental directive to a ten-year-old might be, "Don't watch TV." Consider instead a question prompt, such as the following: "If you watch TV now, will you have time to finish your homework?" Teach children to question themselves: *If I go to the sleepover, will I get enough sleep to play well during the baseball game?* or *If I stay for help after school, will I raise my grade in math?* or *Does this choice help me stay on course toward achieving my hopes and dreams?*

CREATE "FUTURE PULL"

No one has sex to feel good in six months; it is all about the now. Kids need a strong antidote to the pull of pleasure that accompanies their emerging sexuality. Parents must support a strong "future pull" that serves as a compass to get them to their future vision.

At a young age, some kids will have concrete evidence of achievement. Blue ribbons, straight A's, or trophies serve to convey their fledgling sense of worth. Others may have no tangible evidence that they are on track to succeed. However, all young children have a natural ability to believe without concrete proof. Just ask Santa, the Tooth Fairy, and the Easter Bunny.

A child's vision of herself in the future has a powerful influence. The hope to be a surgeon or a pilot will live for some time without proof, but not indefinitely. Along the way, the pixie dust must turn into perseverance, and the vision must be fed by more than just hope.

Over time, more concrete evidence of success will surface. The A in biology or an acceptance letter to a school of choice says "stay on course, you are almost there." Parents should help their kids identify each bit of data that surfaces to make the dream real. Then their *future* will begin to pull them forward.

Creating future pull is a team effort. Kids need to be supported in their attempts to be farsighted and imaginative. Studies show that creative and conceptual thinking can trump rewards and pleasure associated with money and, yes, even sex. An interest or passion that feeds an adolescent's vision of himself beyond the immediate will be a potent factor in the choices he makes.

CORRECTION FACTOR

It happens all the time: a toddler takes two steps beyond Mom and realizes she is not ready for what her little legs will allow her to do. She is trying to get by the boundary of Mom's apron strings ... albeit a little too soon.

It is no different in the teen years. Even if you follow every bit of direction in this book, as they say, *your mileage may vary*. There will be missteps and moments off course. Straying off course is not the problem; it is *how long* your child stays off course that makes the difference. Just because in theory your child crossed a threshold in sexuality does not rob him or her of a successful future.

It is not unusual for a young mind to take a step off its path and use that experience as a marker to indicate where not to go. Just as exposure to a virus is the key to strengthening a biological immune system, psychological immunity develops through testing boundaries. Depending on a parent's expectations and response, kids will either redouble their efforts in the right direction or dig a deeper hole.

Keep in mind that real growth is unstable and at times unnerving. Kids need to know that what they believed to be real or true last month, last week, or last hour could change in a flash. Feeling they were ready for the expectations in a sexual relationship on Friday could all change by Monday.

Year to year, month to month, and in some cases, moment to moment, a corrective factor will need to be incorporated for kids to stay on course. That shift is vital in helping them continue to move toward their true identities and not just what the marketplace pressures them to be.

Remember, our kids will have sexual identities. They may even have great sex. The mistake is allowing sexuality to block the development of the rest of their identities. Walking in a relationship with them that anticipates their sexual development from day one is crucial. Don't just download information. Provide developmental experiences that contribute to the broader story a child tells about himself. With a flood of emotion and new awareness, it is easy for teens to forget who they are and what they want their identities, sexual or otherwise, to say about them. Success requires Mom and Dad to be both message and messenger.

III. HUMAN NATURE
NEEDS NURTURE

INTRODUCTION:
HUMAN NATURE NEEDS NURTURE

HOMO SAPIENS IS THE ONLY species that can adapt to and capitalize on changes in its environment. Our ancestors walked toward the fire and harnessed it to cook their food. And by sharpening stones, they changed from prey to predator. This ability to adapt is as pivotal to our children today as it was for previous generations. However, our modern threats and challenges are less physical and more psychological. Raising kids to feel empowered, understood, and hopeful requires more than a minivan and a swing set.

NOT BORN THIS WAY

It was thought that the discovery of the human genome would provide understanding of everything in us from blue eyes to bipolar disorder. Think of a gene as the condensed potential of a physical attribute or a condition like diabetes. Genes hold a template that directs various proteins to form who we are and what we will look like. There are influences that dictate which genes get expressed and which ones get suppressed. Brown hair wins; blond hair gets voted out. More than a half century later, we may be less of a mystery to ourselves, but we are still very much a puzzle. As it turns out, fewer traits are guaranteed to emerge naturally than originally thought.

These findings shed light on environmental variables that literally act as "switches" to determine which genes get "turned on" and which ones are relegated to the back of the line.

How parents interact with their children can have a profound impact on outcomes during childhood and later in life. Research in epigenetics, the study of outside influences on our gene expression, is rapidly producing a growing body of evidence that suggests early childhood experiences can have a weighty impact on shaping the emotional development of children and their mental health.

Children will need a dynamic response system to work with whatever life throws their way. In my clinical experience, I see clearly that people who are able to productively navigate highly charged moments are the most resilient. When in conflict, they are able to conserve their emotional energy and override an instinct for aggression. Able to remain clear and thoughtful, they use their emotions to connect and create possibilities and avoid dead ends.

Nurturing our kids to gain the ability to go beyond a fight, flight, or play dead instinct is essential to helping them respond constructively to stressors in life. Parents have the capacity to influence children through language, relationships, and imagination, those attributes that set us apart from the animal kingdom.

Studies examining the equation of biology and interaction with the environment are shedding light on why a "one size fits all" parenting approach can leave children more vulnerable to the ups and downs of life. The findings reveal that high pressure and high stress levels for children can easily overload their response systems, which can lead to chronic vigilance to detect threats in their environments, even when there are none.

Pathologies, such as oppositional defiance and conduct disorder, often originate in environments that fail to provide better strategies for responding to highly charged moments. Living with this deficit denies the sensitivities of early childhood experiences. Reacting with defiance can actually be a child's attempt to create safety by not allowing the unfamiliar to reach her.

Every organism on the planet has the ability to defend, and children are no exception. However, a child's nature is ultimately defined by how it is nurtured by caregivers. The notion of a blank slate does not hold up under scientific scrutiny. Neither does the notion of genes as destiny. What does hold up is that the puzzle of who a child will become has plenty of room for possibility if we know where to look.

This entire book has been about getting beyond the low fruit of *nice*, *good*, and *smart*. Parents can offer children a richer path. Through experience and encouragement, we can leave behind the notion of raising kids with fear-based hindsight and replace it with clarity and foresight. Together, families can cultivate habits that bring about our best human behavior and leave the rest behind.

KEEP THE TIGER IN ITS CAGE

It is impossible to move on without some mention of my thoughts on Amy Chua's parenting book *Battle Hymn of a Tiger Mom*. At first blush, the material made me wonder if I had tripped into a time machine. Was it a rehash of moms being blamed for everything from asthma to autism? But after reading more by Amy Chua, I questioned the logic and value of her point of view.

The main parenting tool in her belt is to shame the child by withholding love and affection. Yet, ironically, much of her motive is to avoid being shamed or humiliated by the child's behavior.

American parents are well aware that our children are far more than dumping grounds for our own anxieties. We long ago released ourselves from cords of shame tied to previous generations.

I am often lobbied by parents to enlist support for physically as well as emotionally harsh tactics with children. The campaign quickly reveals itself as a thinly veiled attempt to justify the way the parent's spirit was broken by his caretakers. The numbness that results from surviving such a narrow scope of parenting fosters a similar numbness in the child with regard to her impact on others. Shamed children can become uncompassionate toward others, and rigid and uncompassionate toward themselves as well.

Being asked to live in fear, remain invisible, and ignore personal emotional directives is a textbook recipe for a long list of emotional disturbances ranging from self-harm to clinical depression. Knowing that both are potential precursors to suicide, it should not be surprising to find that the National Institute of Health reports that China has the highest rate of female suicide in the world. Those numbers are based on just the cases we know about.

It may also be worth noting that there is an emerging body of studies being conducted by researchers in Germany that indicate certain neurons related to processing complex emotions, such as guilt and shame, are suspiciously overrepresented in cases of suicide. That's a correlation to consider before throwing your child's artwork on the floor or calling the child "garbage," both events recounted in *Battle Hymn*.

Families craft our instincts, how we learn to respond to threats in our environments. Allowing a child to become comfortable with degrading harshness is just not smart. This can be illustrated in the simple fact that not all people who your child encounters outside the home will have his best interests in mind. But how will your child know the difference?

There is precious little opportunity for "claw back" in parenting. The patterns we wean children on become self-sustaining. The child won't require a harsh verbal thrashing from Mom to feel shame. Over time, he will be able to conjure up the feeling all by himself.

Before the kids re launched, Tiger Moms would be well advised to focus on fostering resilience for the slings and arrows in life that *cannot* be controlled—the fickleness of friends, broken hearts, the changing tastes of an audience, or any number of economic factors that impact the winds of fate.

America is on a path toward innovation and divergent thinking. Sticking to a script that demands compliance from a child at all costs is like psychological cancer. I cringe at the thought of what Ms. Chua would have done with some of the most famous academic underachievers of recorded history, such as Thomas Edison or Richard Branson. Creative outcome cannot coexist with fear or exhaustion. By her own admission, Ms. Chua was a not a reflective student. Terrified to be challenged by her professors, she shared that she remained quiet in class. No curiosity about her studies left her to learn by rote at the highest levels—not a bad thing, but certainly not what the future demands.

CHAPTER 13

Flash Points

Emotions should mobilize, not paralyze.

EVEN TO THE CASUAL OBSERVER, it is clear that today's climate presents a challenge for parents, way beyond ensuring that children "grow up." The challenge is much more related to having a "script to grow." A child will physically grow according to the instructions of her DNA. Her psychological growth is about her capacity to handle complexity, her being able to respond to life's messier, emotional moments in constructive and meaningful ways.

Emotion is the raw material of life and can be jarring to children of all ages. Emotional energy puts us in motion and fuels our growth through everyday ups and down. Getting beyond the surge of feelings that fuel "fight or flight" mechanisms requires skill and reinforcement. Mastering these moments will be a hallmark of well-being in coming decades.

Experiences that guide kids in how to respond to and grow from flash-point opportunities will play a pivotal role in defining who they attract into their lives and how they eventually participate in the lives of others.

Friction is always the precursor to growth. It is part of a natural process to initially push back on the new and unfamiliar. Children's reluctance to engage a new caregiver, brush their teeth, or use a utensil for eating all are signs of friction. Only when the new information makes sense or comes with ease will it be become routine.

During their development, waves of anger, fear, frustration, or even joy will converge with children's thoughts and actions as they push through to new levels of maturity. Children who acquire the capacity to constructively harness their surges of feelings will have a dramatic advantage in life. Integration of emotion, thoughts, and actions will have enormous impact on the extent to which a child is able to meet his needs, develop relationships, and foster his talents.

DRIVING THE FAMILY CAR DRUNK

There is always a basic assumption that because someone made it to adulthood chronologically, her psychological tool belt came along for the ride. Although some parents are emotionally and psychologically better equipped than others, it is rare that such achievement comes without some degree of effortful reflection and consideration.

As the story below illustrates, operating from unexamined emotional patterns is a luxury that no family can afford.

Good Dad Gone Bad

I met Dan after an ugly altercation during which his parents threatened to call 911 if he did not seek help with his temper. His dad was a corporate executive who, for most of Dan's seventeen years, had routinely come home and unloaded his stress on the family. An intimidating figure, he used punishment and fear as his main parenting tactics.

Buoyed by their ability to shut down their child with fear, Dan's parents felt confident in their short-term success. They had not considered the long-term impact of how the humiliation of being afraid would result in repercussions for Dan. His mom and dad were unaware of the toxic brew that was seeping into Dan's perception of himself and the world.

They did not imagine that Dan would one day have his own stressors, that he would find his parents stressful and need to punish their "bad" behavior by using fear and intimidation. Inheriting his father's six-foot-three frame gave Dan a boost of confidence.

Over time and careful excavation of his past, Dan was able to figure out why he responded to stress the way he did. He was angry about all the fear he felt as a child. He knew he was not perfect, but he also knew that his behavior did not warrant being made to feel fearful on a regular basis. This emerging young man also mourned the loss of opportunity to develop a self that wouldn't immediately become terrified when the environment became disagreeable. He wanted to learn an alternative to turning to rage and hurting loved ones.

As we continued to work together, Dan eventually found his punitive father to be as wounded as he was and felt sorry for him. He accepted that his well-meaning parents had unwittingly downloaded a script that taught him to be reactive and aggressive during high stress moments.

Over the course of treatment, we worked to change those patterns. Eventually, Dan became motivated by connecting with people, not dominating them. In time, he came to acquire constructive responses to life's ups and downs. Most importantly, he discovered ways to grow into the powerful young man that he so desperately wanted to become.

Children raised in homes where they feel under threat by a caregiver will self-preserve at the expense of learning and growth. The internal signal that says they are in danger triggers a cascade of chaotic physiological activity. Over time, the chaos becomes the enemy within.

Unregulated emotion compromises brain function as much as several shots of vodka do. When a human being is under threat, the flood of adrenalin and cortisol push brain activity to the "fight or flight" centers in the brain stem. Both have the ability to shut down higher-order thinking. The resulting aggressive behaviors are reflexive and serve to stabilize. Children learn that the only way to feel safe is to respond with aggression, and grow into adults who do the same.

Parents must provide an environment and model that will help propel children to grow. Parents unable to take charge of their own emotional outbursts have little chance of showing their children how to take charge of themselves. Remaining in control of themselves during a highly charged moment is what gives children the confidence to grow.

Prior to language, all we had was imitation to ensure survival. Imitation is a brilliant design when most activity is about dodging predators. For this reason, observing or interacting with a parent during emotional turmoil has exceptional staying power. What children observe and participate in is what they will anticipate in future relationships. If the normal friction that accompanies growth is always misinterpreted as a signal for danger, your child will always respond to that signal as a threat. Our anxious daughters and angry sons pay a heavy price for the missing pieces. Their unregulated emotional reactivity creates useless and destructive patterns. Stuck with a model that only allows for anger and fear, they can easily fall into emotional reactivity that could paralyze a developing mind. Powerless in circumstances that should be safe, they develop an exaggerated vigilance for threats.

BRIDGE TO INTELLIGENCE: A TWO-WAY STREET

Children have a powerful ability to adopt the habits and gestures they observe in their parents. Too often parents mindlessly model the very same destructive habits that they want their children to avoid. When a parent's behavior is reactive or guided by raging emotion, it sends the wrong message. The heat of anger blocks us from taking a closer look at ourselves and each other. Finding the courage to delay reactivity and upgrade emotional experiences is our new frontier; it is a bridge to greater intelligence. Shifting our use of emotion to create opportunity can transform how we teach our children to love and innovate. No child can grow faster than his capacity for emotional regulation will allow. There are no exceptions. The hallmark trait of resilient people is the ability to summon positive energy in the face of emotional stress. People who are able to organize their internal experiences are far better equipped to influence their environments. We also know that they are more likely to be effective leaders, enjoy intimate relationships, and make changes in their lives when necessary, for the better.

In summary, there is no escape from emotional turmoil while raising kids. How children respond to their flash-point circumstances will depend on the options they have available. They need adults to model experiences that teach them to orient themselves constructively, despite being in a highly charged moment.

The key is to nurture and *be* what you want to *see* in your child.

As a parent, you have the most influence over your child's emotional development. Creating the discipline to not be reactive yourself will take time and effort. Remember, the energy of emotion is always trying to find its way back to equilibrium. The key is to nurture and *be* what you want to *see* in your child.

CHAPTER 14

Self-Discovery Is the New Self-Esteem

Self-esteem is valuable, but self-discovery is priceless.

DIAMONDS IN THE ROUGH

THE BEAUTY OF A DIAMOND belies the rough conditions that carbon must endure to give the final product its sparkle and strength. In a process that still retains some mystery, raw materials are subjected to heat and pressure. Strong bonds are created to develop a crystal network. The network grows as each carbon atom is put through the paces to join the crystalline structure. By requiring this hardiness to manifest, diamonds inherently have an advantage. The interaction between raw material and environmental pressures is what ultimately confers their brilliance and strength.

We started this section with a call to collaboration with nature. Through a grand bargain with our genes, our interplay with the environment and certain circumstances will help or hinder humans of all ages to reach their mental, physical, and psychological potentials. Parents play a major role in determining the circumstances their children must wrestle with to become their strongest and most brilliant selves.

As a modern society, we have relied on indicators of giftedness or bolstered self-esteem to secure spots for our children as they ascend the ladder of success. At a time when we cannot risk leaving any talent behind, a closer look at how to proceed broadens the picture and, at the same time, widens the rungs on the ladder.

Parents play a major role in determining the circumstances their children must wrestle with to become their strongest and most brilliant selves.

Our prevailing, conventional metrics for identifying the winners in life will fail the test of reverse logic. Take our popular candidates of parental focus : IQ and high self-esteem. Many of us work off the assumption that a gain in either category would confer larger degrees of success for our kids. When you consider the reverse reality, it is difficult to make the case. Numerous surveys show high self-esteem is quite prevalent among the prison population. Further probing uncovers many people with average IQ scores that have made tremendous contributions to society and lead very successful, satisfying lives.

As independent measures, the traits are admirable. But they may be little more than indicators of good test taking and a high opinion of oneself. As such, they should not be confused with the promise of identifying young people who will thrive in life and love. Nor should they be mistaken for predicting the future masters among our children who have potential to deliver exceptional, original, and inspiring work. Lastly, they have little to do with leaders who can foster cooperation and navigate interdependence for the benefit of all.

CALLING ALL GENIUSES

There was a time in our society when individuality was scarce and conformity was reaching toxic proportions. The opportunities for self-expression were rare and frowned upon. Social upheaval through the decades has rebalanced that formula. Most recently, encouraging our children to express themselves through art, language, and achievement has advanced us in many domains. But times have changed, and even that formula may be in need of rebalancing.

Parents can find themselves caught up in a relentless pursuit of self-esteem for their kids and the "happiness" that presumably follows. In truth, blind faith in measures that address past conditions could be wasting precious time and energy.

We now know from observing, tracking, and documenting our greatest achievers and "would-be" achievers from early childhood that both attributes are actually less prominent pieces of a larger narrative. Continuing to rely on outmoded false prophets, such as IQ scores, to foster the intelligence and promise needed from our future citizens will leave much of their talent on the table. Contributions to society that inspire and rewire a generation cannot be captured in single categories. They require a process.

So a question emerges: if the best and brightest among us are not necessarily born that way ... how do we help our kids get there?

CHILDREN NEED A PROCESS, NOT A PRIZE

The first step is in acknowledging that the formula for exceptional accomplishment may be closer at hand than we originally thought. Second, we must break our belief in the status quo. To thrive in different times requires us to think differently. The pursuit of self-esteem and the anticipated happiness that is supposed to follow have failed to deliver in the end. Parents and kids are more anxious, angry, and depressed than we have been since we've tracked such metrics.

> To thrive in different times requires us to think differently.

Of all the variables our children will be subjected to, the inability to remain energized and robust in the face of environmental shifts or change should be our most dreaded. In our fast new lives, kids today must face challenges that are continually changing the finish line for them. The grand accomplishments that once solidified or guaranteed a path in life are now just invitations to raise the bar.

In some cases, there is a rapid shift in direction without advance notice. Most recently, this notion has probably been echoed loudest in young adults who have hitched their wagons to costly college degrees, only to be dragged down by crushing debt or locked-up labor markets. There isn't enough self-esteem on the planet that could change those realities.

Avoiding this trap may sound like a tall order, but it is not. As parents, we have a huge influence on whether our children can take up this challenge and expand their senses of self. Understanding the difference between self-esteem and self-discovery is a huge first step.

Self-esteem is often the byproduct of an event or a point in time and can depend too greatly on the fickle opinions and goodness of others.

For generations, prizes preserved relevancy. Athletic records, academic achievements, or professional pursuits were tickets to a sense of value or esteem. Today, relying too heavily upon a static moment would be like trying to preserve a single tank of gas instead of devising a way to produce your own fuel.

For kids, knowing the difference is crucial. A growing child's accomplishments are especially vulnerable to the ravages of time. Today, the churn and pressure of societal dynamics make anything that feels static or fixed a bad idea.

Self-discovery is a dynamic process. It is the arrangement and rearrangement of our internal selves. Acting like a template for personal innovation, self-discovery helps children connect to experiences in ways that help them discover more about their own abilities. The resulting self-knowledge fosters self-trust and resilience, which enables them to absorb the naturally occurring ups and downs in life.

Self-discovery is the unsung hero of practically every success story in recorded history. Through the ages, including the ages of the Enlightenment and various inventions, of the Renaissance and various revolutions, every transformational moment for humankind has pivoted on people who had a process, not only when they were winning but, more importantly, when they were losing.

Our most prolific, evolutionary game changers have had something far more valuable than talent and a dream—they have had a template for how to behave when the chips are down. They have somehow found the commitment and grit that provide intrinsic motivation, whether a prize has been close at hand or not. In other words, they have been capable of authoring their own stories and drilling down to their core when external circumstances have not been in their favor. This group has been far from the smartest among us. But they have known that if you fall seven times, you need to get up eight. And without exception, they have been the ones who stay engaged with the problems the longest.

Benjamin Franklin famously said, "I didn't fail the test; I just found one hundred ways to do it wrong." Similarly, Thomas Edison explained, "Of the 200 light bulbs that didn't work, every failure told me something that I was able to incorporate into the next attempt."

That ability, being able to generate energy and motivation in the absence of trophies or applause, is the essence of exceptional achievement and the by-product of self-discovery.

Each of the iconic accomplishments listed below included key people bringing more of themselves to the table when faced with a setback. When their original ideas dimmed and the esteem of others was withdrawn, each discovered and developed a vision from within. That process made a prize unnecessary. The confidence of the comeback did not require specific, predictable conditions. What emerged when the chips were down was an internal fuel cell for the psyche. Each challenge was an opportunity to convert adverse circumstances into fuel for perseverance.

- George Washington lost more battles than he won during the American Revolution.
- Abe Lincoln had infamous political and business failures prior to achieving personal greatness.
- Cornelius Vanderbilt, titan of American industry, did not go bankrupt when railroads eclipsed his shipping empire. He shifted and got on board the train.
- The Wright Brothers did not discover flight; however, they worked with the problem long enough to conquer it. They borrowed from their past experiences tinkering with other machines and motors to help stay on track.
- NASA engineers did not win the first round of the race to space. The Russians and Sputnik did. We stayed with the problem and put the first man on the moon.

Over time and trial, they all acquired a personal infrastructure that animated their journey. To some degree a gift from the gods...in many instances success was crafted from experience with setbacks, loss and failure. They became more adept at *adapting* when things did not go as planned, letting in new information about themselves and their vision. In turn, that process of self-discovery, through sometimes-messy modifications, provided fuel for their journeys. Motivated by this unique turbo charge, they pushed through to new plateaus. They did not look for a finish line—they determined their own.

ADVERSITY, YOUR NEW BF

In his "Self-Reliance," Ralph Waldo Emerson says, "God will not have his work made manifest by cowards." The cultural pursuit of "being happy and problem free" creates a certain unease for most of us. We know on a deep level that we are talking a good game but walking a paradox. The capacity to conquer adversity can produce some of the most gratifying feelings your child will ever experience. A worldview that does not include preparing families for the inevitable randomness and challenges of the world is naive at best. The bill for happiness at all costs will eventually come due. Children untried by the slings and arrows of life will have a difficult time paying it.

Kids need varied and challenging experiences to build a sense of competence. Nassim Taleb, in his book *Antifragile: Things That Gain From Disorder,* refers to this posture of confidence as "antifragile." He advocates that systems, as well as individuals, can learn and grow from stress or the turmoil of adversity. He rightly notes that the optimum outcome for medicine is "dose dependent," and the same applies to stressors that we encounter, physical or otherwise. Taleb notes that the muscles in the human body thrive on being pushed to the next level of resistance. The interaction creates readiness and builds strength.

> **The capacity to conquer adversity can produce some of the most gratifying feelings your child will ever experience.**

The growth and development of children operates the same way. Development is code for change, and children's growth occurs when information is added, not only about people and places but also about themselves. Openness to experience and willingness to engage provide interplay with those circumstances that drive the process of self-discovery.

Young children are programmed to take on physical challenges that will reduce physical dependence on their parents and other adults. Being compelled to walk, talk, or ride a bike changes their perception of the world and adds self-knowledge about their capacity. They do not sit down in smug satisfaction; they clamor for more. The same holds true for their psychological maturity.

CONSISTENT EXPECTATIONS TRUMP GREAT ONES

Over time, the hum of consistent parental expectations will trump great expectations. Building an internal core for growth and autonomy will not arrive with the sound of trumpets; it will live in the silence between directives and doing.

These spaces not only build credibility in parents and their authority but also a belief in the child herself. For example, in that silence lives parental expectations for household chores, approaching teachers about grade discrepancies or clarification, answering the house phone, or being accountable for belongings, all of which are opportunities for building blocks to push over the small hills. By not remaining consistent with the small, we risk leaving a gap for when things become big.

THRILL OF VICTORY AND AGILITY OF DEFEAT

Of course we want children to know the thrill of victory, but it is important to remember that not all adverse situations have claws or teeth. Aiming for "happy" often becomes the default at the expense of discovering the strength or power to cope with adverse situations. Many challenges provide the magic that makes life meaningful and delivers sustained personal pride to the kids themselves, not their parents.

Being familiar with experiences that are unpleasant or even unfair gives kids a better calibration for when things go wrong; otherwise, the normal frustrations of life can feel catastrophic. We will not always be there to guide them. Kids need to have a sense of being able to find their own way when shining moments are few and far between.

Peering into the lives of our leaders and accomplished men and women has long been a pastime that draws many of us to their stories. New findings in the fields of psychology and neuroscience say it is much more than a pastime—it is a vicarious challenge. The autobiographies of others can have a powerful impact on our personal stories. Observing or hearing about challenging circumstances can activate thought and behavior patterns similar to those involved in the action. It explains the very real waves of joy and agony experienced by sports fans, all generated from sitting in a seat!

Remember, the ability to transfer knowledge is a fundamental building block for success for all of us. Without it, we would all be stuck reinventing the wheel every day. The story of others is the story of us; for example, the journeys of elite or professional athletes provide compelling stories, especially for kids to relate to. Let's take a look:

"53"

It is the trial and error of experience that drives life forward despite resistance. Crafting a strategy to respond to the inevitable adversity that accompanies sustained accomplishment is as much a tool in life as a hammer is to a nail.

Moms and dads need to look in the right places for kids to witness self-discovery in action. The problem is that often we pay attention to the wrong things.

Today, we can easily access information about staggering failure or soaring achievement, but the flame that keeps a variety of circumstances moving forward is often hidden in the numbers and between the lines. Experience passed on through biographical stories can help open up the field to show moms and dads where to look.

"Jeter Hits 3,000": by all accounts, this is a powerful number in a powerful headline. This milestone had its humble beginnings with a more formidable foe: 53.

In July 2011, famed shortstop Derek Jeter became the first Yankee to achieve Three thousand career hits. By any measure, it was a remarkable athletic achievement. For kids looking on, imagining themselves in that position is not difficult. Reveling in the roar of the crowd, embracing teammates, and receiving accolades really requires little skill and minimal practice.

However, what they saw was not the entire story that was unfolding. Jeter in his duel with three thousand had a secret weapon. He had what he learned from fifty-three, which was the number of errors he made in his first minor league season after getting drafted by the Yankees. As exhilarating as three thousand can be to the vicarious slugger in us all, without the victory over fifty-three, there is no show.

Even a cursory search for biographic notes on Jeter shows a young man in the minors, uncertain of his talent and in need of support. His nemesis was not the high-speed pitch, it was self-doubt, the urge to ditch and run when accolades and assurances were not there to keep him in the game.

The now-legendary shortstop had to clear that hurdle before tackling three thousand. He figured out how to respond and where to focus when the chips were down. He developed a process to discover more of himself and thereby expand his talent. Even as three thousand approached, the jaws of injury would make him wrestle for it. The steady effort to stay on track was not sustained by the lure of the prize. If it were, we would all pick up a bat. Three thousand never moved a muscle to help; the process he had honed on the way up is what drove him. The confidence seen in him today is courtesy of uninvited adversity that resulted in self-discovery. Children benefit from visible examples of self-discovery in a world that would rather hide it in favor of glitz and glamour.

Jeter's accomplishment may not change the world as Washington or the Wright Brothers did, but it can change our minds about how important a role adversity plays in our modern accomplishments. Iconic, contemporary stories like Jeter's need a second look from kids. Sharing these journeys that zigzag on their way to greatness has the potential to change your children's attitudes and, in turn, the course of their lives.

As kids blaze their own trails and befriend adversity, they are also bolstering their mental health prospects. Psychological immunity emerges the same way our body develops its immune system. A child must be exposed to psychological "pathogens." Experiencing a range of moods and negative feelings will inspire psychological antibodies that come in the form of sadness, failure, and struggle. Natural doses of interactions with those uncomfortable feelings help children develop self-trust and confidence that they can handle some discomfort and still be okay.

No one expects parents to actively seek hardship for their families. However, kids do need to know that they have what it takes to conquer fear and persevere without immediate gratification. Providing space for a sense of self-discovery by wrestling with adversity gives a child proof of her value. It says *I'm alive, I matter, and I can contribute.*

TALENT TRAP

"Mrs. Ferrara, how old are your kids?" Jason was making a casual reference to a picture on my desk.

"They are twins, and they are both ten," I replied.

"I've been playing lacrosse longer than they have been alive, and you know what? I'm done."

Jason, seventeen, had been sent to see me by his mother. She was distraught over his decision to not pursue lacrosse at the college level.

For a kid who was described as rebellious and out of control, I was surprised by his candor and clarity about what was going on around him. Taking a history, I found that Jason had been defined by his talent in lacrosse for most of his life and now felt trapped by it.

He explained his willingness to talk because he needed me to get his parents to listen. He was well aware that he was carrying around their dream, and he was "sick of it." He knew that wins, losses, and awards meant more to them than they did to him. He also knew that he needed to find out what mattered to him. Having a hyper-focus on a single sport left him wondering what else he could do without the pressure of having to be really good at it. He wanted to know when he could make his own mistakes. He reminded me that he wasn't ditching college; he just wanted to do something other than lacrosse.

Kids carry an instinct about their abilities. They know when they are in the wrong lane. Unfortunately, they can find themselves lacking the skills to switch lanes or move the obstacles blocking them.

Underneath his acts of rebellion, Jason is one of the lucky ones. He was able to break out, switch lanes, and explore life beyond his identity as a very talented lacrosse player. Other kids don't always have the instinct to uncouple themselves from their natural talent. They run into roadblocks from parents who treat their natural and healthy desire to road test another skill set as a natural disaster.

Admittedly, there is no thrill greater than discovering that your child has a gift, talent, or ability that can wow a crowd or bring instant status among peers. As families, we end up creating a bubble mentality around a child's pitching arm, academic achievements, or gymnastic feats. In the bubble, parents are tempted to speculate about the child's potential and then relax the rules to take on increasingly higher risks that pay off only in the event that conditions never change and nothing else matters.

Having talent and fulfilling your potential as a person can take place on two different planets. We forget that soaring high is rarely where problems occur. It is when the child must land the plane and live among mere mortals that we see how easily things like athletic achievement can masquerade as maturity. In the absence of that script, many kids crash midflight. Parents can become so fixed on an agenda for their child's talent that they won't let any critical feedback stand in their way. In those cases, the talent becomes a toxic asset because it blocks the child's total growth.

Remember that when a person is trapped by an identity that depends on performance, he becomes less likely to devote psychic resources to other dimensions of himself for fear of appearing weak or not receiving the love or admiration he did when he was performing. Kids with little life experience have trouble filling in the gaps.

The heavy emotional investment of a parent weighs down the child's ability to make a move in another direction. This is what Jason was trying to do. He shared with me his concerns that he did not physically grow as much as the kids he was competing with. They had gotten faster and stronger. Jason knew at some point he would be outplayed. He had a healthy internal appetite to find another way to prove his worth and was willing to venture out and do the work. His parents' agenda stood in his way.

Eventually they acquiesced, and Jason stopped rebelling. He did not need to rebel—he was no longer trapped and was free to leave his talent behind and find a new one.

PARENTAL PAPARAZZI

It's hard to look away. Most parents feel so responsible, hovering around their children, quick to swoop in and assure comfort. We have all had our helicopter moments. Providing too much of a good thing, moms and dads can easily overshoot the mark. Adults end up micromanaging their children, possibly solving one problem but creating many others. Behaving like paparazzi, parents can intrude more than help.

Children need space that is not invaded by prying eyes. Growth can be a messy business. The fits and starts, pauses, and regression involved in raising kids can be unnerving, but they are necessary. Trying to avoid or sidestep the unpredictable often contorts well-meaning parents into habits and techniques that resemble a voodoo playbook of "if this, then that" strategies. Focused on a finished product and guided by narrow assumptions about what their children need, parents can actually block the success that they are so fervently trying to create.

WHEN WE LABEL KIDS, WE LIMIT THEM

Large bodies of research that tracks kids show that a fixed notion of perceiving themselves as "smart" or "talented" can actually hinder a child in terms of larger contributions to society beyond good academic scores or amateur performing arts. Their talent can ostensibly become a trap. Research conducted by psychologist Carol Dweck of Stanford University suggests that teaching kids to think of intelligence and talent as dynamic and malleable can be hugely motivating. In Dweck's findings, it was clear that when a child connects her personal effort to outcome instead of letting the label do the limiting, her achievement prospects rise considerably. Kids almost instinctively connect to their self-discovery process to dig deeper and find more within themselves. Dweck's work shows that knowing that the innate ability is only part of the equation can be a revelation in a young life. In turn, letting go of the labels that limit can create energy to propel kids forward.

CHAPTER 15

Beyond Bullying

BULLYING IS A LIFESTYLE DISEASE that can affect any child. Left unchecked, innocent childhood behaviors can mutate into the cruel victimizing and targeting of others. How, when, and where we intervene are vital factors in determining the outcomes for both bullies and victims.

The headlines about children intentionally inflicting real suffering or pain on each other are sobering and underscore a fundamental breakdown in society.

> Even after a fourteen-year-old boy tragically committed suicide at home in the wake of constant harassment from classmates, the bullying continued. His sister experienced continued taunts during a homecoming dance shortly after the boy's wake. When her brother's favorite song was played, friends chanted his name in a display of support, but the very bullies who initially harassed him were relentless, chanting "You're better off dead!" and "We're glad you're dead!"
>
> Other headlines describe high school students behaving like sexual predators, in which digital photos depicting the

horrible act of sexually assaulting a classmate were posted for public perusal. Her attackers became "digital grave diggers" by intentionally creating viral circumstances so shameful for the victim that she ended her suffering by ending her life.

The behavior of our kids toward each other is sometimes so egregious that it is impossible to ignore the specter of mental illness in the making.

We have spent a lot of psychic energy preventing our kids from becoming victims. Parents have employed everything from bulletproof backpacks to anti-bullying pep rallies. But those measures only serve to protect children from the bully's blow. While some of these efforts are successful, they are not sustainable.

The only real solution is to tackle the core question: *How do we prevent kids from becoming bullies?*

The surprising truth is that unsuspecting, well-meaning parents are raising a generation of bullies. They are unintentionally neglecting to introduce the critical skills and attitudes necessary to prevent their kids from developing a bullying mentality.

It comes as no surprise that parents don't want a child, especially a boy, to be perceived as weak. Some are convinced that such a label would doom their child to lose in the game of life. While not true, there is such negative social stigma attached to the perception that parents may bolster their child's position of strength to such an extent that he goes too far in the opposite direction.

In other cases, parents look the other way when their child behaves in an overbearing manner. Some children live in environments of neglect, where they have no guidance and gravitate to the wrong end of the spectrum. Even those who have done their best to raise caring children can be blindsided when they discover that their kids are, in fact, bullies.

Whatever the case, the transformation doesn't happen overnight. It's a gradual process that, left unchecked, feeds upon itself and grows like a cancer. Just as it's easy to conceive that a young pickpocket may progress to committing grand larceny as an adult, it's not a stretch to consider that a youngster who gets away with pushing kids around in kindergarten will rule the playground in elementary school and dominate the high school hallways by using force and fear.

UNDERSTANDING THE BULLYING MENTALITY

A bully is not born. A bullying mentality is developed through repeatedly violating boundaries and not receiving intervention at early stages. A teenaged bully has probably already committed a decade of boundary violations. The core of the problem stems from a child who lacks options, or has been deprived of them.

Some children seem to have a tendency toward aggression. While a parent may not have taught her child to smack, Mom (or Dad) also may not have mitigated the behavior in previous circumstances and offered an alternative.

Lack of early intervention is the leading factor that cultivates bullying behavior. Intervention can be effective as early as age three, when language is emerging. That's where we need to apply the brakes. Every parent must have a major stake in eliminating bullying. We need to understand how the systematic progression toward interpersonal aggression between kids occurs, identify it in our children at its earliest stages, and halt it.

BULLYING BEHAVIOR HAS RISEN TO
A LEVEL OF PATHOLOGY

Studies show that certain people feel pleasure or reward from seeing others in pain. We live in a culture that carelessly desensitizes our youth and does not provide support to recalibrate acceptable levels of empathy, cooperation, or both. Such psychological deficiencies can be *hallmark traits of a sociopath.*

But by allowing intentional, repeated, and uninhibited cruelty, are we raising part-time sociopaths? It is not a question meant in jest. The traits sound eerily familiar to those of a sociopath. Psychopaths are born with a lack of ability to relate to the emotional well-being of others, but research indicates that sociopaths are made. Genes intersect with environmental factors to create fertile ground for sociopathic tendencies. Exposure to detrimental lifestyle factors, such as neglect, abuse, and aggression, affect developing minds with varying degrees of impact. In other words, a person can be "a little sociopathic" depending on his environment. The lifestyle issues are controllable; therefore, a lifestyle mental illness can not only be controlled but prevented. We have to control the factors that we can.

Children who enter adolescence without adequate amounts of empathic experiences to help shape and curb their appetites for reward will be more likely to advance their behavior to cause pain to others. Just as young athletes are trained to reach their potentials, children with aggressive tendencies will be directed by how we respond to early infractions. Research also shows that direct intervention early on can completely change the outcome for youth with aggressive tendencies.

We must develop a new intervention model that prevents us from creating environments that cultivate bullying behavior.

Adolescents are compelled by their DNA to try to position themselves with alpha dog status among their peers. If channeled negatively, the outcome can be disastrous; however, if harnessed and directed constructively, it can serve children well. Children need to take risks so they can discover where their power lies. Feeling powerful is a big part of healthy growth and development, but it crosses a dangerous threshold when one child victimizes another in order to achieve that feeling.

We must change the climate that feeds the temptation to exploit the weak for pleasure and risk the pain of others for personal gain. With lives at stake, we no longer have the luxury of hindsight.

As a society, we have reduced murder and mayhem in our biggest cities following a simple premise: if you identify the hotspots and concentrate your crime-fighting activities, you curb the progression of crime. The criminal's specter of being caught is a powerful deterrent. Stopping the progression of a young bully is no different from curbing the petty criminal's transition from misdemeanor-level crimes to felony-level crimes on city streets. It doesn't require more manpower; it requires good strategy. Identifying the problem spots, whether on the bus, in the locker rooms, or in cyberspace, is the first step.

BULLIES VS. COWARDS

Cowards have few options in life. When clouds gather on the horizon, they take cover under their umbrellas and flee. Hijacked by fear, a coward never stops to consider if the coming storm might bring in not only rain and wind but a rainbow of opportunity and options in life.

Bullies are consumed with the same fear but react differently. Relying on an attack response to fear, they stick around and get drenched, using the umbrella as a weapon or shield. Saving face at all costs is their modus operandi.

It is a well-known fact in psychological circles that the greater the threat, the more primitive the response. In both scenarios, fear is the motivation for response. Drawing from their limited, primitive menu of response options, the bully chooses "fight" while the coward chooses "flight."

Both the bully's and the coward's potentials to grow beyond reflex are held hostage by their fear. An attitude born of fear and inexperience is dramatically heightened during adolescence.

Bullies are unable to take even the slightest risk to be vulnerable and not belong. The belittling in which a bully engages is insurance for belonging and rising in the social food chain. It is a guarantee against loss of status ... or so she thinks.

Expert hostage negotiators know one thing for sure: the only way to influence another person is to understand the motivations for his beliefs and behaviors. Get that wrong, and you are in the weeds. Without similar understanding, you have little shot at influencing children. Trying to end bullying by telling children to "be nice" or hanging anti-bullying signs in school gymnasiums is no match for the challenges kids face today. They need confidence and clarity about what to accept and what to reject from others. Children are like heat-seeking missiles, continually scanning the environment for subtle cues on how to proceed. Families and communities must take the time and effort to *resensitize* our youth to personal boundaries.

Hit-or-miss strategies won't work, so it's our critical role as parents to get it right and influence children from the start to circumvent the bully mentality. Too often we are misguided by relying too heavily on teenage bystanders to intervene and thwart a bullying attack. Teens are already an unpredictable population, so the likelihood of getting a kid with the foresight and emotional support to intervene and diffuse a random bullying situation is slight. Getting beyond the bluster of a bully requires well-designed experiences and cultural support from the adults on duty. It is our obligation to create an atmosphere where kids can feel powerful in ways that do not cost someone else her dignity and, in some cases, her life.

THE POWER OF EMPATHY

As a matter of scientific fact, we are born not only to compete but to cooperate, care for one another, and understand one another, a trifecta that begins with the care and understanding of oneself and the ability to relate to others. Helping children develop empathy is the pivotal tool. It's much more than just being nice or feeling sorry for someone; it's an acknowledgement of shared experience and feelings. Empathy is an act of courage that begins with the ability to tolerate our own feelings of discomfort and connect that to another's experience.

We can help children develop empathy by providing the language to relate and reflect, which will ultimately strengthen their internal senses of self. The trick is to capture those neural connections and give them the most airtime and exercise. That, in turn, makes them stronger. The connections made early on are far reaching and can even influence your child in a remote location. For example, if you teach a child the ABCs at the kitchen table, they won't be forgotten in a classroom. The same principle applies to the capacity for empathy. Empathy "wired" in the backyard will certainly translate to the schoolyard and beyond.

Children must be reached before the storm of adolescence blocks the inroads for parents and other caring adults. Parents must invest time and nurture children persistently with an effort that rivals how we train our little leaguers and valedictorians. That same gusto must be applied to helping our kids develop the skill set that creates empathy in school hallways and beyond.

THE LANGUAGE OF EMPATHY

As we know, some people derive an innate sense of reward when seeing other people in pain. As an increase in personal advantage is perceived when they inflict pain, children are likely to take on more unexamined risk to reach the reward. Replication emboldens, and if they are allowed to repeatedly violate, the risk becomes diminished, allowing the cycle to continue with no end in sight.

Consumed with the fear of appearing powerless, children are attracted to the immediate rewarding feeling that bullying provides, and they become accustomed to that "quick hit." Parents can stop the cycle by consistently offering a convincing replacement for the quick hit that a bully craves. A repertoire of positive, constructive, and empathic behaviors is the antidote. Empathy provides a powerful feeling of connection that will trump any feeble, short-lived reward derived from bullying. Guiding children to the language and skill of empathy helps them develop strong, rewarding relationships with others. In turn, they can feel better about themselves.

At a minimum, empathy can neutralize the compulsion to forcibly take someone else's dignity. At best, it can totally eliminate the threat. That ability rises and falls with the capacity of language to describe internal experience, which can occur as early as age three. Once acquired, that skill will become an internal backstop for causing harm to another. So where do we get it, and how do we keep it?

As attentive and validating parents or caring adults, we must help children articulate what their motive or fear is and give them an alternative coping mechanism that is equally convincing.

When children discover they can manage to stand on the edge of a disagreeable, highly charged moment and not attack, they encounter the possibility to grow. When someone acquires the language to identify that he is fearful, he has a relatable data point for fear. When he finds himself in a situation and understands someone else is afraid, his previous experience allows him to understand and relate to it. That connection is what will help him do the right thing.

See Spot run.

See Spot bite Jane.

See Jane cry.

See Dick hug Jane.

The mental processing required to create Dick's empathic behavior and the act of reading the sentence about his behavior are based on the same principle. The difference is that creating brain circuitry enabling someone to read the sentence is close to a miracle. The actual act of empathy requires no such miracle. We are born with the capacity for empathy.

During a child's first five years, opportunities exist to amplify traits of kindness and empathy that can be built on through early adulthood. "Be nice" has been the catchall directive for kids since the beginning of time. Regardless of the offense, "everybody play nice" has been the tried and true parental directive. But is it really the issue? Is someone not being nice, or is it that she is not being empathic? It's a vital question in light of the mountain of research that points to empathy as the definitive backstop to inter-child cruelty.

Previous generations developed empathic skills more readily as a by-product of their environments. Our work and home environments bred the personal contact and connections that required more dependency on one another. That is no longer the case today.

Language about our internal experience is the bridge to relating to someone else's internal experience. We can't wait for an incident to prompt the conversation. We must engage in dialogue with children consistently. The key is to preempt problems, and the earlier the better. When there is conflict between the child and his environment, that is the ideal teaching moment to start to write a script for the child to identify what is going on for him and proceed in a way that is constructive and not destructive.

Eruptions are common between kids: "Mommy, John pushed us off the raft while we were playing on it!" "Daddy, Dylan kicked me on the way home from school!" Does any of this sound familiar?

In each case, the offenders did not have the basic skills to monitor themselves and then express their real needs. Just as learning basic arithmetic skills is critical to comprehending complex math concepts down the road, teaching children how to accurately communicate basic information about their feelings and emotions is an essential precursor to developing empathy.

Interventions that help children build the language to identify what is motivating them internally will go a long way toward avoiding and diffusing conflict with other kids. Once they are able to articulate their own needs, they can more readily understand, identify, and empathize with the motivations of others. This will eventually serve them as adults when they engage in higher-stake relationships.

If John had developed the ability to articulate what he really wanted, which was simply to play with the other children, he could have overcome his fear of rejection and wouldn't have had to tip the raft.

A quick inquiry would have revealed that Dylan provided a kick to indicate his annoyance that his sister took the last PopTart' at breakfast earlier that day. If he had been primed with an alternate behavior, such as asking her to split the treat, his delayed physical response could have been avoided. If his sister understood the power of empathy, she could have responded to that wish in kind.

In each situation, the solution is based on providing positive alternatives. It's a matter of repetitive mastery, gaining the language, gaining self-awareness, and nurturing the rewarding feeling of empathy.

A parent can prompt a child by asking what she needed or wanted when she erupted. It's important to lead with the word *what* rather than *why* to promote a thought process that will assist the child's concrete ability to reflect about what happened.

For example, if Jason hits his sister, ask, "What did you want?" Your child can focus quickly on his wants and articulate them, such as, "I wanted to watch the Disney Channel."

If you ask, "Why did you hit your sister?" it's less likely that you will get to the core of the matter. Children don't necessarily know *why* they want something, but they do know *what* they want. Instead you might elicit a less helpful response, such as, "I don't know; she kept changing the channel." Only by asking what he wanted will we learn what Jason wanted to accomplish. Then we can provide him with an example of how to use language to express his desire to watch a particular show.

Our job is to help children develop and use language to articulate their needs. Keep it simple. As they get older, they will be more able to express the why. This phase is the precursor to expressing their needs when their identities become more complex.

The next step is to help them learn how to employ empathy to understand the other's point of view. The process is leapfrogged over in bullying instances. The worst offenders need the most help to understand themselves and their behaviors. Kids who bully need an opportunity to reflect on their own feelings and experiences before they can be successful at recognizing the feelings of others.

CYBERBULLYING

What we can't see can't be that harmful, right? Wrong. The truth is, technology has made bullying just a keystroke away.

Most adults over forty who use technology have spent decades strengthening their ability to read how their words and actions impact others. It was not until the recent decade that they began to live in a virtual "coffee klatch." Many had already developed a well-honed radar that has helped them guide and craft electronic messages. No such luck for our children! Youth of today are not getting a chance to cultivate interpersonal skills. Just at a time when they should be striking out on their own, they encounter technology's offer of anonymity, isolation, and speed—a poisonous combination and breeding ground for abusers. They can act on impulse and get immediate satisfaction without accountability. Technology is the first step in creating a wall to hide behind, and a means to get away with their crimes.

Human beings were designed to live in a physical world, and we are wired from birth to tune into how we are impacting those around us. Ninety percent of our communication occurs non-verbally and unconsciously. A furrowed brow or flushed face can tell volumes about how another person is feeling. A signal of fear or sadness will have an immediate impact and help recalibrate both parties' responses to avoid aggression. Without the benefit of *face-to-face feedback*, interpersonal communication among teens can become the "Wild West" without rules or boundaries. Texts, e-mails, or social media posts can short-circuit the empathy and reflection skills necessary to deter bullying.

The Internet is non-discriminatory. It can be as much a tool for humanitarians as it is for pedophiles or bullies. *Cyberbullying* among youth is on the rise and *intensifying*. In previous decades, the role of alpha dog turned bully was reserved for the physically strong. With the advent of technology, teens are using the power of these tools to flex their virtual muscles. Where physical proximity was once a requirement to become a bully, technology has ushered in an era of equal access and opportunity to harm without restraint. Kids eager to play with different identities are using the virtual world as a playground for power.

Teens are living increasingly secret lives, and technology is enabling that. Parents and school administrators can no long consider cyberbullying a "spectator sport." Putting tools with such power in the hands of teens without any accountability is like letting preschoolers have unsupervised access to the cafeteria knives and then being surprised when someone gets hurt.

The first thing any abuser does is isolate the victim. In isolation, all problems seem more overwhelming, and it's often the reason why many cyberbullying victims do not share the problem. Face-to-face intervention can diffuse situations, but a *non-personal* medium of communication circumvents any chance of natural intervention. Unchecked, communication can progress from constructive to destructive in a keystroke.

A lot rides on how we help our children build their relationships with technology.

The solution is to *prepare our children to navigate the online world.* A lot rides on how we help our children build their relationships with technology. Research indicates that children who are at risk of having difficulties online also struggle offline. Your child's individual level of readiness to deal with difficult situations offline is a good indicator of whether he should be allowed to communicate online via the various social networking platforms.

Make sure children understand what a cyber attack looks like. Many are unaware that they are victims of bullying or actually guilty of victimizing. Recognizing the spiral nature of cyber attacks is critical to stopping them. Being prepared gives your child a template for how to respond. Knowing what to do gets things back on track quickly with minimal damage.

Parents must keep emotions in check and respond in a constructive, positive manner. Get the facts, and show your children where they could have made better choices. Explore the mistakes and consequences of their peers' experiences as well.

Let kids know who the adult resources in their lives are, including parents, teachers, coaches, or extended family, who are able to offer help.

At first the vigilance may seem extreme, but the death of a child due to cyberbullying is tragic, and we have no choice but to prepare and protect our children from harm that is difficult to see until the damage has been done.

BANISHING THE BULLY: GUIDING PRINCIPLES

While prevention is the ideal solution to bullying, it's important to protect children when bullying does occur. These principles serve as guidelines to identifying, addressing, and diffusing bullying situations.

Bullying Is a Lifestyle Disease

Early detection of bullying is key. Behaviors in children as young as three or four years old can give clear signals that early intervention is required. Prevention during early stages of development offers the best chance for success.

Beware of the Homegrown Bully

Parents or siblings may unknowingly model bullying behavior for younger children. If a child feels powerless in the home, she will create her power on the playground.

Bullying Is about Creating Victims

Bullying is a way of securing power in the world by victimizing others. It is a behavior that is often motivated by insecurity or an inability to come up with another way to communicate.

Teach the Language of Empathy

We can help children develop empathy by providing the language to relate and reflect, which will ultimately strengthen their internal senses of self, eliminating the likelihood that they will victimize other children.

SWAT Team Response Is Needed for Bullies and Victims

Early intervention is a must. Bullying starts out as a habit based on opportunity. Parents and caregivers must supervise at a proximity that allows for timely redirection before actions tip the scale to victimizing.

Create Predictable Home and School Response Policies

Identify which adults and peers are *resources*. Predictable enforcement of consequences will discourage bullying behavior. Dependable adult backup will encourage victims to stand up for themselves.

THE NEW 3RS—RESPOND, REFLECT, RESOURCE

Learn how to *respond* robustly. Children need a script that tells bullies that their behavior is not going to work.

Prepare a variety of responses. Different situations require different tactics. Make sure your child has several alternative resources.

When possible, use the opportunity to *reflect,* teach alternate responses, and reinforce the use of empathy. Punishment poisons. While the first instinct is to punish the bully, punishment is useless in creating empathy. Punitive measures only serve to inspire a revenge-oriented cycle of bad behavior.

We can help children get on the right path by giving them options. If we can help them *reflect* on the flash points that trigger their bullying behavior, and if we can give them the language to identify those triggers, we can help them recognize alternative reactions and solutions.

We need to provide every child a script for resiliency. They need the capability to ask, *What do I need? What is the real outcome I am after?*

CHAPTER 16

Guns a' Blazin'

I am a rock; I am an island. And a rock feels
no pain. And an island never cries.

—Paul Simon and Art Garfunkel

WE HAVE ALL SUFFERED WHILE reading heartbreaking headlines describing senseless shootings, some closer to home than we would ever have imagined. Places once preserved for safety, such as movie theaters, schools, and malls, have all served as backdrops for mass violence. The killers, who end or destroy their own lives in the process, make these heinous acts incredibly difficult to comprehend.

Forensic psychologists do their best to explain the behaviors, citing minds tortured by paranoid schizophrenia, psychopathic personalities, or suicidal depression that could spiral out of control and into mayhem. Problematic genetic profiles combined with access to automatic weapons are surely big factors in the equation, but they are in no way the entire story.

Reactionary emotional references to "evil" are not helpful. They make this issue seem entirely too supernatural and thereby beyond our sphere of influence.

The circumstances of these rampages are real and complicated, and finding answers will not be easy. Research indicates that we must do our best and work with the odds. That means we need to reduce the odds that our children feel so mentally unstable and disconnected from humanity that a massacre seems like a viable solution to troubled times.

Delving into the issue of violence requires that we reach beyond the question of how to protect. As parents and guardians, we must find the courage to ask, "Will my child become the shooter?" It is vital that we get past this as hypothetical. It must be treated as a reality.

Research already shows that certain environments and influences make violence more likely than others; we just have to believe it. We must own the possibility that the forces that drive our children to emotional extremes could be largely of our own making. More and more unspeakably violent acts are being committed by people in our communities who are not completely mad or already on a "most wanted" list. Many are children or young adults at their breaking points. Often they are kids in need of rescue from the abyss of mental illness. If society is to keep our children safe, it is more urgent than ever to be able to identify potential trouble before it escalates and winds up on the front page.

MORAL IMAGINATION OF VIOLENCE

Now is the time to allow ourselves to explore the unthinkable. This reality check is our first line of defense. Improving our collective understanding of how the day-to-day experiences in the lives of our children either build resilience or tear it down is paramount.

If I ever found myself or my children under real threat, I would be relieved to know that I could summon the energy and focus to fight back for their survival as well as my own. Ironically, this capacity for violence, to protect with force, is a double-edged aspect of the human condition. In many cases, people who commit violent acts often only differ from you and me by degrees. Acts of violence are not general behaviors from certain people. Violence is more likely to be a specific endpoint that can be reached by anyone. Morality is not the issue. To rage into violence, at its core, is self-preservation. Research has shown that under the right circumstances, or the perfect storm of fear and turmoil, we all have the potential to act outside of our rational selves.

Mental health clinicians also know that latent capacities for all kinds of issues, including addictions, anxiety, and violence, can coexist with favorable qualities in our psyches. They can live in harmony with our abilities to laugh and love … until the environment calls them into action.

Even in the face of all we don't know about people who commit these acts, there are a few things that we do know. It is a mistake to conclude that mental illness is the cause of wanton violence. Clearly it is not. The majority of those afflicted, when properly diagnosed and treated, live productive, peaceful lives.

We also can be sure that the acquisition of weapons does not directly translate into murder. The will to kill does not appear overnight. Born of biology as much as a set of beliefs, violence is an extreme act of aggression fueled by rage that is often initiated by experiences that create intolerable powerlessness.

Obviously, mental imbalance will play a role in any act of such an extreme nature. However, mental disorders occur in degrees and follow a progression.

Identifying signals for emotional disturbance early on is critical. Just as we live with and manage factors that contribute to other threats, such as epidemics, chronic disease, and drunk driving, precursors to mental illness require the same vigilance and intervention.

DOING THE RIGHT THINGS REQUIRES THAT WE ASK THE RIGHT QUESTIONS

Not long ago we had only a primitive understanding of many diseases. Our comprehension of much of our cognition, mind, and neurobiology remains rudimentary; however, we are making strides. Advanced tools, longitudinal studies, and genetic research have helped us identify and understand precursors to undesirable outcomes later in life. Research clearly shows that even kids who may be genetically vulnerable to pathology can be protected from the progression of an emotional or behavioral disorder with the proper intervention.

Expert analysis concedes that trying to predict who will resort to a violent act on innocent bystanders is a futile effort, but we cannot ignore that there are emotional components that stand out as common threads among those who have pulled the trigger. This is especially true among school shooters.

Isolation and troubled relationships were often the calling cards. In each instance, the shooter suffered from a profound sense of alienation. The shooters perceived the world as a punitive place and externalized the blame for all of their pain. Chronically frustrated, each one had difficulty navigating the social landscape. Sadly, the shooters believed that everyone was against them. Over time, to ease the blow, these kids cultivated feelings of contempt. Dehumanizing the people around them made their acts of violence that much easier.

Dehumanizing the people around them made their acts of violence that much easier.

Educators, mental health professionals, community members, and parents do not need to be experts to ask the right questions. Just by reducing our fears and increasing our skills, we can open up opportunities to intervene. Being aware of some basic principles of childhood development as it relates to mental health are the first steps to intervention. The sometimes powerful, informal, and communal care provided by grown-ups can make a world of difference in the trajectory of a child's life.

SOME OF THESE KIDS ARE NOT LIKE THE OTHERS

Some of these kids feel as if they just don't belong. It is important to acknowledge that some kids find it more difficult to engage the world. A combination of biology, environment, and culture will serve to either support or delay a child's developmental progress. When plagued by various social struggles, children get fewer opportunities to craft positive identities or build confidence.

Research indicates that there are some social tendencies that could make a child more vulnerable to mental health challenges than others. As is often the case with developing minds, detecting early signs of vulnerability and distress is the best defense. Studies indicate that the quality of emotional communication received in early childhood will have a dramatic influence on the child's well-being. In many cases, it will be the strongest protection a child will have against vulnerability to mental health issues.

BLIND SPOTS

No one can know exactly why a person would choose to harm or murder defenseless men, women, or children. It's nearly an impossible task to predict which of our children will one day act out in violence. What we do know is that early intervention is critical because deteriorating mental states are very difficult to retract beyond adolescence. At the same time, we must resist the urge to dehumanize people whom we deem capable of violence. By labeling them, we avoid our societal responsibility to constructively intervene.

The Columbine school shooting best illustrates this very real and vexing problem. The killers had radically different mental conditions at the time of the shooting. One was depressive, suicidal, and prone to emotional outbursts. He was hurting on the inside. The other, after years of forensic investigation, was conclusively identified as a psychopath. Cool, calculating, and homicidal, he was unable to relate to the feelings of others due to his minimal experience with engaging a range of emotions himself.

Both struggled with the social and sometimes cruel landscape of adolescence. Their adolescences were peppered with marginal connections and frequent bullying episodes in which they were the victims.

Their appetites for violent entertainment certainly could have played a role as well. The evidence shows that while a culture flooded with violent images may not move the needle on a child who is not prone to aggression organically, kids with aggressive tendencies will certainly be emboldened. Such exposures give them traction for violent methods to channel aggression. In other words, they can easily be caught in a contagion of "copycat" behaviors.

Still, neither profile gives society license to condemn people with similar profiles as mass murderers in advance of an act of violence. In the absence of a checklist to tell us for certain which children will harm themselves or commit an act of violence against others, our job as parents is to be better informed and provide positive influences in a young person's life.

The eyes and ears of primary caregivers and adults in a child's life are well positioned to track and redirect habits and traits early on in their development. Adults must become more adept at identifying kids who are stumbling in their developmental journeys. Gaining knowledge to be better at identifying patterns in a child's life is crucial for effective, proactive interventions. Without it, children trending toward despair or prone to violence will live in our blind spots until a blast of aggression or act of violence announces their arrival.

FEAR FACTOR

We are closer to understanding certain conditions that predispose kids to aggressive spirals in behavior. Child-rearing practices that help kids respond constructively to stressors in life can have a profound impact on their mental health. We know from studying brain mechanisms involved with aggression and violent behaviors that how a developing child is able to regulate his emotions will go far in helping us recognize signs of trouble. Research shows that that if his reflexes are primarily based on fear (real or imagined), aggression is more likely.

By all accounts, human babies are born into this world as distressingly chaotic little creatures. They are fearful as they try to process a milieu of signals and sensory input. Their brains are furiously building fibers of connection to sort out friend or foe. In time, those connections will form the circuitry for moving, thinking, empathizing, and planning, among other abilities. The soothing touch or calm demeanor of an adult helps modulate the frenzy. The role of a parent is paramount in assisting children to be able to process incoming stimuli and respond in a nonchaotic, thoughtful way.

Over time, a baby's brain begins to become less aroused by sensory input. These initial social interactions begin the process of quelling the more primitive parts of the brain. The newly sparked neural fibers are essential to coordinating with signals from other parts of the brain. Maturation is incremental and depends on the stability of those fibers and the connections that eventually form.

The more these neuronal connections are used, the stronger they become in a cycle of amplification. That is why we should stimulate the ones we want our children to be guided by most often.

Interactions and physical contacts between caretaker and child build a neurological "levee system." This is the beginning of the psychological infrastructure that keeps a flood of fear stimuli from washing out other fragile cognitive connections that are trying to gain use and strength.

The budding connections to language centers will begin to quiet the noise of "fight or flight" that leads to aggression. As "self-talk" emerges to self-soothe, children's behavior becomes less impulsive and more thoughtful, enabling verbal signals to gain muscle. The strength of these thinking areas, unlike the lower primitive ones, is deeply dependent on environmental influences.

We can easily see this in a two- or three-year-old child who feels threatened when a playmate approaches her toy. Her fear is directed primarily by her reflexive, primitive brain. Her weakly coordinated thinking areas will not stop her from biting or hitting in response to the perceived threat. Later in development, that same child, bringing language on board, will be able to override aggressive impulses by saying "no" or "stop."

The same applies when the immediate distress or fear from Mom leaving the room triggers a primitive outburst. Over time, these reactions are curtailed by the acquisition of language. A signal is relayed that says, "I'm okay; she'll be right back." The rewards of self-soothing recruit more cells for connection. Bigger cognitive pathways are built to compete with fear-based, primitive impulses. If the child is supported by attentive adults, the process of emotional regulation based on thinking can begin.

These experiences are critical for a child to avoid developing habits of aggressive behavior when he becomes afraid. Parents must ensure that children become successful at generating positive, flexible thoughts, *especially during moments of fear.* The goal is to provide equal amounts of strength for the various brain areas.

If things go well, neuronal connections and coordination are established in one area of the brain and then develop in the next, a pattern that continues with each coming month. Patterns of self-regulation begin to settle the chaos and minimize the loud signals of fear. That resulting personal emotional stability is a critical precursor to sustained mental health and cultivates feelings of personal power. The child is able to take in new experiences without being hijacked by fear or overwhelmed by new stimuli. This *dynamic stability* delivered through parent/child interactions enables children to enter the world with less fear and more connections.

STAND BY ME

Sadly, for many kids this progression is not always simple or guaranteed. Each of us is born with a unique baseline of how we process incoming information.

Some children have a "feelings center" that runs a little hotter than those of other children. Even in the absence of threat, their threshold for a "fight or flight" response is low. These kids are quick to feel aroused, as if under threat, and react. Whether the information is visual, verbal, or otherwise, that baseline determines how intense our emotional response will be to stimuli. Efforts to think are lost in a flood of negative, fear-based sensations. Fragile thoughts trying to make connections for comfort are unable to crystallize. Negative emotions take over, driving the child out of control. Subsequent outbursts leave the child confused and disconnected from friends and family.

Young kids with neural circuitry that skews toward anxiety or fear need more support in their growth and development. Prone to outbursts and highly reactive, they have tremendous difficulty remaining stable and relaxed in the face of incoming stimuli or stressors. Most parents don't even know that they are responsible for strengthening the "settle down" signal in young kids. Unwittingly, they often engage in the exact opposite. Adults frequently exacerbate the problem by responding to an emotional outburst from a toddler or teen with their own chaos. Kids with a highly reactive baseline become increasingly fearful. That added environmental stress *triggers and strengthens* the wrong cycle, inhibiting the rest of the brain.

This is a critical point when it comes to understanding aggression. It is well documented that underdevelopment of brain areas that modulate behavior will increase the odds that a child will respond to uncertainty with aggression. This is especially true as her world becomes more complicated and stressful in adolescence and young adulthood.

It is not difficult to imagine how exaggerated responses to feelings of fear can create a range of problems in a young life. Brain systems, intended to self-preserve, go into overdrive. It becomes tougher to suppress unproductive reactions. Left uninterrupted, much of how the child responds to life will be based on a heightened awareness of threat. Cycles of anxiety, fear, and depression begin to feed on themselves. Instead of connecting with the world, a child's internal state makes him feel as if he must continually defend himself from it. Such an irrational spiral of thinking can make everyone the enemy and therefore, in extreme cases, everyone a target.

LOVE ME … LOVE ME NOT

Kids who struggle with sensitivities and the emotional complications that follow can present a real and difficult challenge. Parents are unable to put their fingers on a tangible reason for meltdowns or refusals to cooperate. This is especially frustrating when siblings, being raised by the same parents, breeze through situations that trigger outbursts in another child. The slight of a friend, being late for school, or the chaos of a middle school social scene can present real challenges for kids who are easily rattled.

Year after year, more and more parents seek guidance for children whose level of anxiety or degree of emotional outbursts is seemingly inexplicable. As a counselor working with these families, I see clearly that these children possess exquisite sensitivities as a part of their native intelligence. Many have a high degree of competency in more artistic realms. The budding visual artist, an eye for design in architecture, a strong connection with animals, or intense interest in technology is exhibited.

These children, destined to *resensitize* this world, are actually too fragile for their hostile environment. Forcing them to navigate a 24/7 culture filled with messages of violence, greed, pornography, and hypocrisy may just be asking too much for these more sensitive kids.

These kids have difficulty experiencing the warmth and connection that engaging the world with open arms can bring. The most salient consequence for these kids is a compromised ability to feel loved. At the mercy of their primitive response systems, they are unable to participate in the essence of love—to share themselves with others emotionally.

For children who are highly reactive to their environments, the uncertainty of social exchanges can often result in anxiety. It is easy to see how their inability to self-regulate could make maintaining stable, positive interactions very difficult. Without help, they will struggle to remain open to the positive rewards that social connection provides. Over time, they can easily become habituated to a negative bias toward social interactions. Unsure and fearful, many of them look to isolation as a way to cope.

The absence of social connections for a child is a sign of trouble.

The absence of social connections for a child is a sign of trouble. Inability to have positive social contact can lead to profound feelings of powerlessness and alienation. Without positive social investment, kids often turn to aggression for connection.

REDUCING ODDS REQUIRES RELATIONSHIPS

In his book *Real Boys*, William Pollack writes, "Violence is the final link in a chain of disconnection." All children must make the journey from "me" to "we." It is the only way for them to meet the most basic human need to belong. Their earliest relationships provide the seeds of dignity and value necessary to move into the world. These social connections provide the initial confidence that must take hold before they are faced with finding their own way outside of the watchful eyes of Mom and Dad. Each child needs to be supported at a pace that works for her.

Providing opportunities and experiences to successfully engage the world through healthy relationships is by far one of the most protective factors for children and their mental health. It is through relationships that kids will be able to repair themselves when hurt or find the courage to self-discover.

Effortful participation with the people around them provides the initial cords of what sociologists call a "stake in the community." That investment not only positions other people as valuable but gives the child a platform to have those positive sentiments reflected back. Cradled by those connections, he gets the confidence to expand himself and invest more effort into others.

In the absence of support, kids often find it easier to retreat. Missing early developmental windows for acquiring a comfort level with social interaction can be a dire mistake; this is especially true if the child struggles with emotional regulation. When a child is younger, remaining alone has little consequence other than just being alone. However, parents fail to consider the biological and psychological forces that will begin to apply pressure as the child transitions through puberty and young adulthood. We underestimate the confusion and jarring emotions that easily make a sensitive child chronically agitated and more fearful than before. The safety of solitude will no longer provide the satisfaction it once did.

These kids, accustomed to being alone, will no longer be able to avoid the call for acceptance by the outside world. The ensuing inner chaos can create internal conflict that spills over into the family room. Poor understanding of these psychological drives can make kids seem even more unreachable to befuddled parents.

MY BAD

Kids who become aggressive or even violent are not all the same. The prevailing notion that they don't like other people is not true; the problem is that they cannot tolerate the anxiety of connecting with other people.

Over years of working with children and their families, I have learned that their unruly behaviors can mask their anxiety to form relationships. In a tinderbox of loneliness, existing pathology can be exacerbated. It is also quite possible that preventable mental health issues, such as depression, anxiety or addictions, can begin to emerge.

These misunderstood children continue to break more relationships than they make. As they grow older, they are painfully aware of this cycle yet completely at a loss for how to fix it. Time and again, they recycle destructive instincts and make things worse. They feel victimized and are at maximum capacity for pain. Unable to take on more, they begin to project all blame outside of themselves. That effort to sidestep the sting of accountability is very costly. They miss the rewarding process of personal responsibility.

It is the comfort of relationships that allows kids to accept blame when they have made mistakes. In isolation, without the assurances that loving relationships can bring, there is a lack of objective feedback or guidance. Their stress is no longer caused by external circumstances; it is entirely subjective and internal and therefore difficult to escape. Hostility toward others can seem like their only option to protect themselves and conquer their fears.

BUILDING BOUNDARIES ... BELIEVING IN CHILDREN

There are kids who can navigate the social ropes with little support or direction; however, that is not the case for many. In situations where children struggle to remain open to social connections, it is important to remember that they will need to do more work with less comfort.

The value of social rewards can be lifesaving for a child. Remaining with her stride-for-stride to ensure she experiences the benefits of social interaction is key. This makes success in family relationships critical. Conditions at school or on the playground may not provide sanctuary for a child who is overwhelmed. In the home, with family members, may be the only place where she feels safe enough to spread her fragile wings and grow. The parent-child relationship is exceptional in many ways. No other relationship will carry the opportunity and influence that a parent will have on a child. Your relationship with your child is the only way to monitor and modify her budding sense of self-control. It is the primer to comprehending and processing emotions like love and disappointment. Relating to your child, giving her the willingness to walk in the shoes of another person, is vital. Steady support will give her confidence to take on more complex relationships. How our kids live their lives will reflect who we were to them.

Increasingly, our children's worlds will become interconnected and interdependent. Interdependence will require far more than texting or tweeting; children will also need to be capable of soliciting support for themselves. Just as teaching kids good hygiene and a healthy lifestyle can shift the odds of succumbing to the flu, understanding relational skills can have equally good outcomes for their mental health. Learning how to behave with boundaries and relate to friends and family can buffer kids from the unpredictable in life. The challenge of ensuring that each child has protections for his mental health is no different than the challenge of making sure each child learns to read. With awareness and proper support, mental health is well within our grasp.

FOUR FACTORS TO REDUCE THE ODDS OF AGGRESSION
Stop Normalizing Isolation

Allowing kids who struggle with emotional regulation to escape to virtual worlds for hours on end is a problem. Already predisposed to difficulties navigating the social landscape, these kids must have as much practice with face-to-face contact as possible. Unsupported by a sense of community, a developing child can find it hard to access comfort after disappointment. The resulting loneliness sets up a vicious cycle that often leads to more escape. The stimulation provided by gaming is especially counterproductive to the thoughtful regulation these kids need. Without sufficient exposure to the natural ebb and flow of being with another live human, relationships can become too taxing for these kids, and isolation becomes their protection.

Prioritize Emotional Regulation

Ensuring that children can regulate their emotions during stressful moments may be the single greatest legacy for mental health you can bestow upon them. The ability to remain connected and engaged during moments of disagreement or fear is by far the best buffering against aggressive tendencies. Remember, the ability to regulate emotions is required to strengthen the cognitive signals responsible for problem solving and relational skills. Each time those cognitive signals override "fight or flight" impulses, they are ensuring their own well-being for years to come. If a child continues to struggle to build self-control into middle childhood, that is a clear signal that professional intervention should be considered. Mental illness may not be indicated at present, but the patterns could create obstacles to maturity and subsequent developmental damage.

Stop Sibling "Stuff"

The influence of family members is unmatched in a child's development and sense of well-being. What goes on between siblings is not just "stuff." It matters. Research shows that a child's self-definition later in life could be as closely tied to her sibling connections as it is to parental influence. In a world where so many variables are out of our control,

getting a handle on sibling strife is a must. Sibling relationships are po-
tentially the longest relationships your children will have in their lives.
In many ways, siblings provide kids' first reflection of themselves outside of the adoring eyes of their parents. This is where kids experiment
with how to manage and respond to the world.

Poorly monitored interactions between siblings can be detrimental,
especially for a more sensitive child. These experiences will carry into
how they perceive themselves in the world. Constant conflict for status
in the family has no upside; it will only encourage resentment and feelings of isolation in the exact places that kids should feel connection and
understanding. Too often exchanges are allowed to spiral to ugly places.
Verbal comments, insults, humiliating gestures, or damaging property
are repeated violations of physical and psychological spaces for a young
mind. In some cases, if the power differential is great enough, the activity could rise to the level of abuse.

Depending on the behavior, targeted children could easily come
to anticipate aggression or being victimized. This sets a poor model
for their outlook on life. Such trauma could leave them vulnerable for
a variety of mental health issues. Kids often make poor choices in the
absence of a better script. Setting sibling boundaries about acceptable
behavior should be a priority of every home environment.

Relate to Them

Parents must be more than safety managers and material pro-
viders to the family. We must help children cultivate habits of connection. Just as we were designed to physically move, neuroscience
confirms that we were also designed to be emotionally connected to
each other. When healthy interpersonal connections fail to form in
childhood, aggression and violence have a breeding ground. If kids
are not primed to pursue the rewards of pro-social give and take,
their drive to survive will take a negative form. Little hands with the

potential to help and hug will mutate into hands that hurt and harm just to feel connected.

The nature and quality of our relationships with our kids will be barometers for what our children can expect from the world. The ability to feel safe, loved, and understood is delivered through relationships. When parents engage kids and relate to them, kids feel encouraged and understood. An attentive adult can provide containment for feelings that might otherwise prove overwhelming.

Providing language to process and problem solve promotes investment in others. When a child shares his experiences, it makes him feel less alone. It is also how a parent can track a child's psychological and emotional progress. Negative biases or rising anxiety can be detected, monitored, and addressed.

IV. RELATIONSHIPS BUILT TO LAST

CHAPTER 17

Longevity: The New Peer Pressure

*You are the bows from which your children
as living arrows are set forth.*

—Kahlil Gibran

A LONG LIFE SPAN IS one of the unique and most intriguing traits that humans possess. Whether by medical miracle or many miles logged at the gym, it is a trend that will continue well into the twenty-first century. Longevity creates great potential for the opportunity to share many years with our children as peers. It also presents a challenge that represents a much different landscape than our grandparents could have anticipated.

Not long ago, most of child rearing was focused on preparing our kids to live with someone else. Young women were groomed for husbands and marriage. Men were prepared for education, the workplace, and supporting a family. It was a simpler time when parents had influence that loomed large and cast a long shadow. Relationships and influences outside the family circle were rare. Once our children completed college, got a job, or tied the knot, our work was done.

Times have changed. Today's world floods our children with options and influences that make an imprint that can permeate and surpass the influences of their families. Just two generations ago, shorter life spans would not allow for parents to live and see the fruits of their labor. They were also mercifully saved from having to live with their sometimes poorly conceived legacies and mistakes. For the most part, we will not be able to sidestep ours. With average lifespans rising to surpass eighty years for many, the future for our families will be very different. Parents will have the chance to enjoy their children for many decades as adults. We are shaping the very people who will emerge as our colleagues and cultural leaders. We will live to be led, governed, entertained, protected, and cared for by our kids.

This gift of time and purpose after our reproductive and childrearing years is new and uncharted territory. Releasing the pressure to produce a prodigy, we must attune ourselves to the pressure of our longevity—not only behaving today in a way that leaves a legacy with our children, but actually living it with them.

Showing up with the title of "Mom" or "Dad" will not have the caché it once did. An unexamined rehash of old expectations is not enough. We will not be able to escape our failings. They will fall on our children. And we will live to see where we skipped and hopped instead of planned and protected.

We now know that we must raise kids to do more than just pay their bills and do their laundry. They must be prepared to create and participate in relationships and real life. It is time to imagine yourself without the trappings of power over your kids (money, keys to the car, food, roof over their heads, etc.). As our children eventually become the new generation of entrepreneurs, lawyers, politicians, parents, or bosses, our roles as parents will shift dramatically. We will be working and living side-by-side and interacting with them as peers. For this new relationship to succeed, we have to be willing to cannibalize our outdated power base *before* outside influences do it for us.

Ultimately, our job is to raise children in a way that provides them with the tools and traits necessary to navigate their journeys into adulthood. At the same time, we must prepare them to be able to connect and relate to us in ways that preserve their dignity, and assure ours, throughout this new and very long life with our offspring. It is only through our understanding of the precious opportunities we have with them as children that we can make sure they see our value. That critical connection will serve as a beacon for them to find their way back after they launch into the world.

Our children will be able to give to us as well as we gave to them. It is not enough to expect a relationship with your adult children. We must prepare them for it.

Looking both ways is crucial. We must determine which parenting influences to bring forward and which should be left behind so that we may collectively guide our children. Finding the courage to ask if we are weaving a narrative for their futures or replaying an outdated version of our pasts is a good start.

CHAPTER 18

9 Evolutionary Principles to Parent with Possibility

THERE WILL NEVER BE A singular magic formula to transform and protect our children through their developmental journeys, but there can be better understanding of how to parent with clarity and sustainability.

The goal is to expand on the things that are helpful and sidestep those that are not. We can't possibly know everything about how our children will be influenced or challenged, but we can learn basic fundamental truths that drive behavior and guide our society. As our world becomes more complex, it's more critical than ever to achieve clarity about the dynamics that drive outcomes. Derived from the patterns of human behavior, these nine principles can help us focus our efforts, give us confidence and direction, and serve as anchors, especially when the chips are down:

1. Consistency creates credibility.
2. Friction always precedes growth.
3. Perseverance breeds success.
4. Self-reflection is the foundation for empathy.

5. Language skills level the playing field.
6. Emotional regulation is the key to resilience.
7. Play is the precursor to innovation.
8. Interactions must be scalable to be sustainable.
9. Self-discovery creates self-esteem.

These principles are designed to give our children the framework to reach their potentials and bring their gifts to the table, even in challenging circumstances. They give parents a platform to stay engaged throughout a process that not only serves their children but helps enhance their own well-being as well. Parents can confidently build upon these principles to guide desirable outcomes, create constructive environments, engage in meaningful dialogue, and respond with intention rather than react.

Parents are the key to success. As we embrace our opportunities, let's look both ways—at ourselves and at our children—to open up a world of parenting with possibility and confidence. Let's examine the experiences of our past, evaluate the results, and bring forward what works. We will leave behind what doesn't, and we will lean in with imagination to support the futures of our children and all they touch throughout their lives.

The Beginning

BIBLIOGRAPHY

BOOKS

Berninger, Virginia, and Todd L. Richards. *Brain Literacy for Educators and Psychologists.* San Diego: Academic Press, 2002.

Bilton, Nick. *I Live in the Future & Here's How It Works: Why Your World, Work & Brain Are Being Creatively Disrupted.* New York: Crown Business, 2010.

Csikszentmihalyi, Mihaly. *Flow: The Psychology of Optimal Experience.* New York: Harper Perennial, 1991.

Erickson, Eric H. *Identity and the Life Cycle.* New York: W.W. Norton & Co. Inc., 1980.

Gladwell, Malcolm. *The Tipping Point: How Little Things Can Make a Big Difference.* New York: Little, Brown and Company, 2000.

Gleick, James. *Chaos: Making a New Science.* New York: Penguin Books, 1987.

Godin, Seth. *Linchpin: Are You Indispensable?* New York: Penguin Group, 2010.

Healy, Jane M. *Failure to Connect: How Computers Affect Our Children's Minds—and What We Can Do About It.* New York: Simon and Schuster, 1998.

_____. *Your Child's Growing Mind: A Practical Guide to Brain Development and Learning from Birth to Adolescence.* New York: Broadway Books, 2001.

Hill, Napolean. *Napoleon Hill's Golden Rules: The Lost Writings.* Hoboken: John Wiley & Sons, Inc., 2009.

Lynch, Gary, and Richard Granger. *Big Brain: The Origins and Future of Human Intelligence.* New York: Palgrave Macmillan, 2008.

Maeda, John. *The Laws of Simplicity.* Cambridge: MIT Press, 2006.

McKibben, Bill. *Enough: Staying Human in an Engineered Age.* New York: Henry Holt, 2003.

Newman, Katherine S., et al. *Rampage: The Social Roots of School Shootings.* New York: Basic Books, 2004.

Ramo Cooper, Joshua. *The Age of the Unthinkable: Why the New World Disorder Constantly Surprises Us and What We Can Do about It.* New York: Little, Brown and Company, 2009.

Robinson, Ken. *Out of Our Minds: Learning to Be Creative.* West Sussex: Capstone, 2001.

Scharmer, C. Otto. *Theory U: Leading from the Future as It Emerges.* San Francisco: Berrett-Koehler, Inc., 2009.

Seigel, Daniel J. *The Developing Mind: How Relationships and the Brain Interact to Shape Who We Are.* New York: Guilford Press, 1999.

Taleb, Nassim Nicholas. *Antifragile: Things That Gain from Disorder.* New York: Random House, 2012.

Turkle, Sherry. *Alone Together: Why We Expect More from Technology and Less from Each Other.* New York: Basic Books, 2011.

ARTICLES

Boyce, W. Thomas and Bruce J. Ellis. "Biological Sensitivity to Context: I. An Evolutionary-Developmental Theory of the Origins and Functions of Stress Reactivity." *Development and Psychopathology* 17 (2005): 271–301.

Choi, Charles Q. "Suicide Cells." *Scientific American Mind* 12 (December 2011): 15.

Chua, Amy. "Why Chinese Mothers Are Superior." *Wall Street Journal* 8 January 2011. Accessed 22 March 2012. http://onlineWSJ.com/article/SB10001424052748704111504576059713528698754. html.

Cloud, John. "The Myths of Bullying." *TIME* 12 (March 2012): 41–43.

Costello, Victoria. "A Mind in Danger." *Scientific American Mind* (March/April 2012): 31–37.

Cullen, Dave. "The Depressive and the Psychopath." *Slate.com* (20 April 2004).

Dobbs, David. "Beautiful Teenage Brains." *National Geographic* (October 2011): 37–59.

Fields, Douglas R. "White Matter Matters." *Scientific American* (March 2008): 54–61.

Freedman, David H. "The Perfected Self." *The Atlantic* (June 2012): 42–49.

Gaidos, Susan. "Physicists Join Immune Fight: Principles Beyond Biology May Help Explain How the Body Battles Infection." *Science News* (January 2011): 22–25.

Geary, David C. "Primal Brain in the Modern Classroom." *Scientific American Mind* (September/October 2011): 45–49.

Gopnik, Alison. "How Babies Think." *Scientific American* (July 2010): 76–81.

———. "What's Wrong With the Teenage Mind?" *The Wall Street Journal*, 28 January 2012. Accessed 29 January 2012. http://online.WSJ.com/article/SB10001424052970203806504577181351486558984. html?..

Herbert, Wray. "On the Trail of the Orchid Child." *Scientific American Mind* (November/December 2011): 70–71.

Higgins, Edmund. "The New Genetics of Mental Illness." *Scientific American Mind* (June/July 2008): 41–47.

Klebold, Susan. "I Will Never Know Why." *O, The Oprah Magazine* (November 2009): 161.

Mantell, Ruth. "Beware College Students Carrying Credit Cards." *US Edition of Wall Street Journal* (10 September 2012): R2.

Reicher, Stephen, and S. Alexander Haslam. "Culture of Shock." *Scientific American Mind* (November/December 2011): 57–61.

Stosny, Steven. "Lions Without a Cause." *Psychotherapy Networker* (May/June 2010): 27–53.

Subotnick, Rena F., Paula Olszewski-Kubilius, and Frank C. Worell. "Nurturing the Young Genius." *Scientific American Mind* (November/December 2012): 50–57.

Summers, Nick. "Why Winners Win at ... The New Science of Triumph In Sports, Business, and Life." *Newsweek* 18 (July 2011): 46–48.

Sykes Wylie, Mary. "As the Twig Is Bent." *Psychotherapy Networker* (September/October 2010): 55–58.

_____. "Mindsight." *Psychotherapy Networker* (September/October 2004): 29–39.

Taylor, Marisa. "In Praise of Failure." *Ode* (October 2008): 42–48.

Zimmer, Carl. "The Brain." *Discover Magazine* (June 2010): 26–27.

ABOUT THE AUTHOR

Early in her career, licensed therapist and parenting strategist Tricia Ferrara, MA, noticed a couple of trends among parents, regardless of how old their children were. First, parents were under enormous pressure to have their children gain personal advantage. Second, despite a growing body of useful information being generated by researchers and scholars, parents were woefully under-informed about childhood development, leading them to squander opportunities to enhance their children's ability to grow and learn.

Tricia heeded the call to fill that gap—to help parents get the critical information they need, when they need it—and has redirected countless families and helped keep them on course through her straightforward, principle-based approach that gives comfort and guidance to parents with children of all ages.